BLESSING POWER OF THE BUDDHAS

Norma Levine now lives in England, but spent five years in a Himalayan monastery. She has travelled extensively in India and Nepal, and is an expert on Buddhist art and sacred ritual objects. She has practised Buddhism for more than twenty years.

Blessing Power of the Buddhas

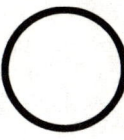

SACRED OBJECTS,
SECRET LANDS

Norma Levine

ELEMENT
Shaftesbury, Dorset • Rockport, Massachusetts
Brisbane, Queensland

© Norma Levine 1993

Published in Great Britain in 1993 by
Element Books Limited
Longmead, Shaftesbury, Dorset

Published in the USA in 1993 by
Element, Inc.
42 Broadway, Rockport, MA 01966

Published in Australia in 1993 by
Element Books Limited for
Jacaranda Wiley Limited
33 Park Road, Milton, Brisbane 4064

All rights reserved.
No part of this book may be
reproduced or utilized in any form or by any means,
electronic or mechanical, without permission in
writing from the Publisher.

Cover illustration by Diane Barker
Cover design by Max Fairbrother
Designed by Roger Lightfoot
Typeset by Footnote Graphics, Warminster, Wiltshire
Printed and bound in Great Britain by
Redwood Books, Trowbridge, Wiltshire

British Library Cataloguing in Publication
data available

Library of Congress Cataloging in Publication
data available

ISBN 1-85230-305-0

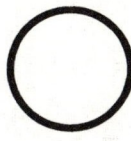

Contents

Introduction   1

PART I: Sacred Objects: Empowerment, Revelation, Expression   7

- I   The Body of the Buddha   9
- II   Images of Ultimate Truth   21
- III   The Womb of Origination   35
- IV   The Limitless Expanse   51
- V   Spontaneous Expression   67
- VI   Buddha Activity   87

PART II: The Hidden Lands of Padmasambhava: Gateway to Wisdom Mind   103

- VII   Journey to the Heart of Light   105
- VIII   Dissolving the Boundary   123

Notes   137
Glossary   139
Biographies   144
Bibliography   151
Index   153

List of Plates

Plate No.
1. *Kutshab* of Guru Rinpoche in *lima* metal from the *terma* collection of Chokgyur Lingpa.
2. Stone Buddha in the Sarnath Museum, India, dating from the reign of King Asoka.
3. Dusum Khyenpa (1st Karmapa): the statue which taught the six yogas of Naropa.
4. Two Buddhas made from *naga* clay by Nagarjuna.
5. Footprint in stone of Guru Rinpoche emanation at the old monastery at Rumtek, Sikkim.
6. The bone of the 16th Karmapa from which a buddha has formed spontaneously (*rangjung*). Sacred relic at Tsurphu Monastery, Tibet.
7. One of the five principal *kutshabs* of Guru Rinpoche.
8. Clay *kutshab* of Guru Rinpoche with his two consorts, Mandarava and Yeshes Tsogyal; from the *terma* collection of Chokgyur Lingpa.
9. Bell and *dorje* belonging to King Trisong Detsen (eighth century); from the *terma* collection of Chokgyur Lingpa.
10. *Namchak* (sky metal) *phurba*; from the *terma* collection of Chokgyur Lingpa.
11. *Namchak* (sky metal) *dorje*; from the *terma* collection of Chokgyur Lingpa.
12. Egg-shaped relic of the Buddha.
13. *Rangjung* Green Tara at Asura Cave, Nepal.
14. Handprint in stone of Guru Rinpoche, outside Asura Cave, Nepal.
15. Baudhanath Stupa, Nepal.
16. The inner hidden land of Tashiding in Sikkim.
17. Khechuperi: sacred lake formed spontaneously in Sikkim.

The Twelfth Tai Situpa

We are in an era of great discoveries, and one of the consequences of the rapid advances of science and technology is the widening of each individual's horizons.

We have liberated many boundaries.

One of the most important elements for development is getting to the heart of the issue through an accurate and direct means.

This book, *Blessing Power of the Buddhas*, will serve to open up and clarify Vajrayana Buddhist culture, philosophy and principles.

I believe this book will be of great benefit.

With my sincere prayers,

The 12th Tai Situpa.

DEDICATION

*To the spiritual activity
of the glorious 17th Karmapa
and the 12th Tai Situpa,
and the perfect rebirth
of HE Jamgon Kongtrul Rinpoche.*

ACKNOWLEDGEMENTS

Many great Lamas have contributed their wisdom to this book. I would like to acknowledge, with gratitude, the great kindness of the following: His Holiness Dilgo Khyentse Rinpoche and his attendant, Matthew, His Holiness Sakya Trizin, His Eminence Tai Situ Rinpoche, His Eminence Gyaltsap Rinpoche, the late His Eminence Jamgon Kongtrul Rinpoche, Dzongsar Khyentse Rinpoche, Beru Khyentse Rinpoche, Chimed Rigdzin Rinpoche, Chokyi Nyima Rinpoche, Sogyal Rinpoche, Tarthang Tulku, Thinley Norbu Rinpoche, Sangye Nyempa Rinpoche, Thrangu Rinpoche, Karma Thinley Rinpoche, Ugyen Tobgyal Rinpoche, Yeshe Dorje Rinpoche, Chokling Rinpoche, Chaktrul Rinpoche, Tenga Rinpoche.

My thanks also go to Dodrupchen Rinpoche for the text of the Lhatsun History; to Lama Setchou for his description of Pemako, and Lama Tsering for his of Ah Ja Ling; to Diane Barker for her painting on the front cover; to Sally Forwood, Linda Gaboriau and Shenpen and Mike Hookham for their comments on the typescript; to His Holiness Shoko Asahara for his translation of the Prophecies of Guru Rinpoche, and Jeremy Russell for his help in obtaining it; to Ward Holmes for his photograph of the bone of the 16th Karmapa; to Peter Roberts for help with translation; and to my editor, John Baldock, for his supportiveness.

I would especially like to acknowledge the unremitting encouragement of Tai Situpa, who blessed this book with his time, energy and inspiration.

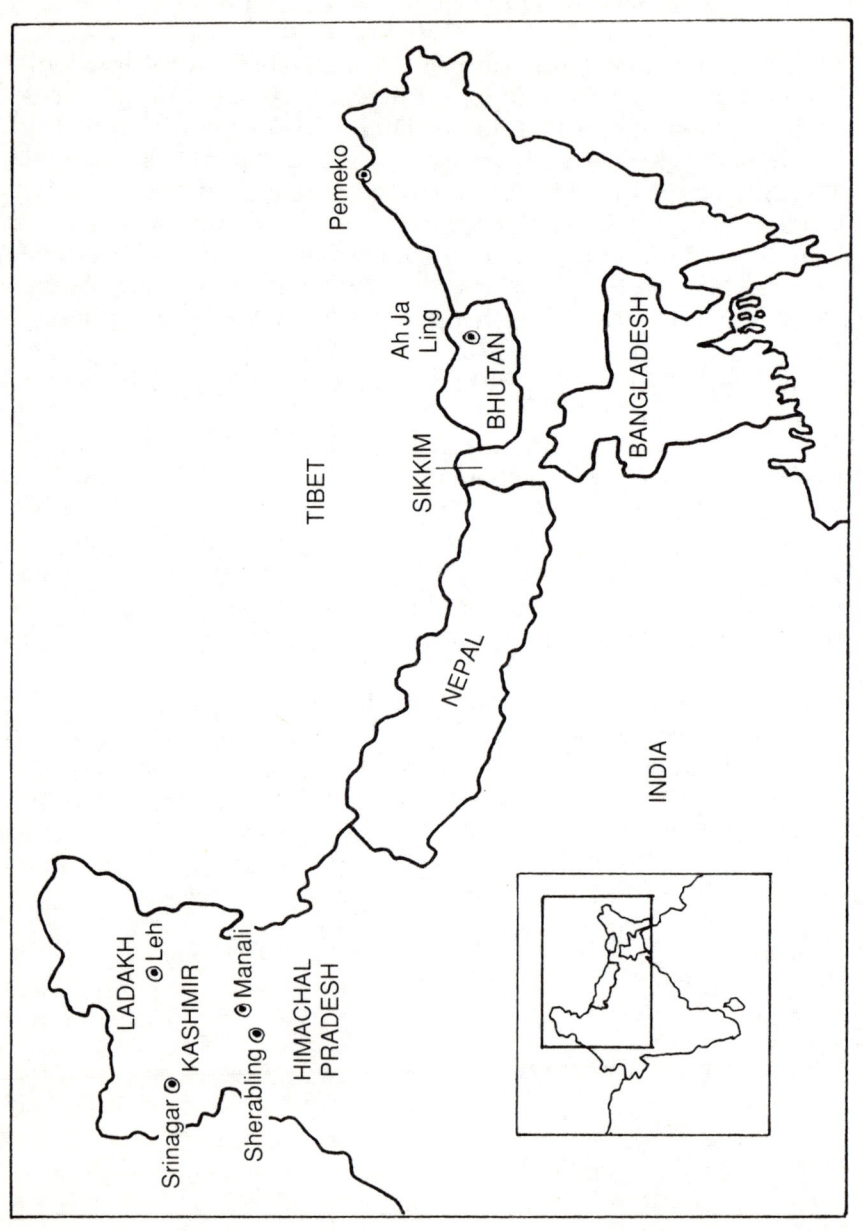

Introduction

The most accessible and universal expression of Buddhism is the image of Sakyamuni Buddha adorned in simple monk's robes, one hand holding a begging bowl, the other touching the ground. Inward turning, simple, grounded in serenity and renunciation, it is evocative in its primal, timeless purity and awakens our longing to retrace our steps back to the roots of our own being.

For me its most magnificent expression is in the stone figure of the Buddha sculpted in the Golden Age of Buddhism, the reign of King Ashoka, now resting serenely in the Sarnath Museum near Varanasi in India. Perhaps it is the proportions which are so perfect that it draws us to our own heart centre, or maybe it is the beauty of that serene, gentle inner smile; but when I saw it everything in me stopped and I wept tears of recognition. I recognize that state because it is part of my own being. It is our buddha nature and that image, carved by an anonymous stone sculptor in the third century is making us *wake up. Do it.*

Or do nothing. Is there anything to do? It looks so simple, can't we just sit there and *be* like that? The truth is, it *is* simple, but we, unfortunately, are not. For most of us our path is through the labyrinth of our own convoluted being. So to retrace our steps means to connect with the blessing power of the buddhas and enter the pure dimension of experience.

As a Tibetan Buddhist practitioner for the past twenty years, I am deeply interested in sacred objects. The first one I owned – briefly, as it happened – brought about a memorable experience which altered my perception about everything. Fifteen years ago, on my first trip to India, I was wandering through the narrow twisting maze of ancient pathways in Old Delhi bazaar and entered an antique shop. From the shelves crammed with exotic statues in intricate poses, I selected a simple Tibetan copper statue of Sakyamuni Buddha. The metal was dark, worn with time, and somehow warm.

I returned to Dharmsala and shortly afterwards received a letter that changed my life. There were simply a few brief words of advice from a Tibetan lama I had met in Scotland: 'if you have any questions about *dharma*, go and see Tai Situ Rinpoche', he said, and he gave me the address of his monastery near Bir in the Kangra valley bordering Dharmsala. The name Tai Situ startled me. For some inexplicable reason I felt joyously excited at the prospect of meeting him ... again; for it seemed more like reconnecting with an old friend than meeting a stranger. I literally jumped on the next bus heading in the direction of Bir, taking the Buddha statue with me to be blessed.

By the time the bus halted it was nightfall, the sky showed a dark thunderous face as the first monsoon rains gathered, and I had no idea how to reach my destination. Bir was the end of the line in every sense, a tumbledown Indian village plonked in front of the spectacular Dhauladhar mountain range. I took temporary refuge from the sudden downpour under a jagged overhanging tin roof, trying to ignore the covert glances of a small group of grinning, self-conscious youths. Suddenly a clear-eyed, serious boy appeared from the night and offered his help. The next morning under a hot blue sky he guided me on the long winding forest road to *mandir* – the temple – to find 'jungle Lama'.

I could appreciate the significance of the nickname. Sherabling was five miles away through a hauntingly wild pine and rhododendron forest, although I could see pumpkin-coloured mud-walled farms and lush paddy fields on one side of the road. Vultures the size of farmyard geese took off from the treetops overhead with a great whirring of wings, circled slowly and landed with a thud. Far away I could hear the scream of jackals. I loved the smell of the hot pine forest and the deep, evocative silence. At midday, joyous, I arrived.

I was shown into a simple room with an old man sitting on one side and a young man on the other. The old man looked peaceful, but the young man was luminous. He beckoned me towards him. At this first meeting with Tai Situpa we talked for two hours like old and close friends. I told him of my plan to go to Ladakh in a few days, and he told me he was also planning a trip to Ladakh

Introduction

that summer. We agreed that I would wait in Srinagar for his jeep to arrive and join his party on the dangerous mountain road to Leh. I took out the Buddha statue and asked him to bless it. He filled it with various substances, intoned mantras with accompanying hand gestures, blew on it, sealed it, and handed it over to me. Brimming with blessing from our wonderful meeting and jubilant at the prospect of a journey together, I took off the next day for Srinagar in the vale of Kashmir, to wait. The mountain peaks and Buddhism of Ladakh lay enticingly ahead.

Kashmir turned out to be a confusing mixture of green sensuous beauty and wolf-eyed stacatto-sharp bustle. I swam languidly in the lotus lakes, beckoned to the shikara-boats laden with luscious fruit and drifted into a tranquil haze like Ulysses lost in the land of the lotus-eaters. The journey to the post office was the single event of the day and after a month of nothing my hope dried up. Languidness turned to boredom and boredom jolted me finally into action. I resolved to board a bus and go alone. Any day now ... soon.

To my great dismay, I had completely lost my nerve. I foresaw a terrifying journey in a dilapidated Indian bus up a sliver of snake-like road. After a week of dread, I forced myself on to the bus, taking the single front seat to the left of the driver. It was, as expected, an expressive display of ingenious third world recycling incorporating windows that neither stayed open nor fully closed, seats with iron railings, in which you could neither sit up straight nor slouch comfortably, for the railing would get you either way, and a colourful, bold shrine which dangled and fluttered from the driver's mirror, cluttering his view through the front window. My small, worn army rucksack with the Buddha wrapped in cloth carefully packed inside it came on board with me – that and 400 rupees was all I had so I focused my attention on it. Behind me was an old Ladakhi peasant, his gnarled hands fingering prayer beads as smooth and worn as pebbles in water. At the very back of the bus was a group of French tourists in new camping gear. There was the usual cluster of street-wise Kashmiri antique dealers, middle-class urban Indian tourists with their tiffin sets packed with delectables, and timeless Ladakhi country folk in woollen tunics and fantastic hats studded with turquoise and coral chunks, taking their first step in the modern world. There was no obvious group to ally with so I braced myself for the two-day journey to Leh. The buses always travelled in convoy on this, the 'most dangerous road in the world', but that was hardly reassuring.

We soon left the lush ripeness of Kashmir, ascending the eerie moonscape of magenta and orange rock over the 16,000 ft Zoji-la pass into Ladakh. A hair's breadth away from the bus wheels the road plunged into emptiness thousands of feet below. I looked down and gasped. Splayed out far, far below was the wreckage of buses, trucks, jeeps. Vultures and eagles circled in the crystalline sky overhead, then swooped downwards out of sight. Not a land for humans, I thought. A ten foot high figure of Maitreya Buddha in the dust-gold rock stood as gatekeeper to the land of the gods. Reassuringly our driver pulled up, got out quickly and made his prayers before driving on.

As we were winding our final arduous way down from the pass, the bus in front lurched suddenly out of control, ran crazily for a short distance, crashed into the mountainside and overturned neatly. It turned out that the brakes had failed — my nightmare was turning into reality. So we stopped, pulled out the passengers — miraculously all alive — and slept on the road overnight. In the morning the army came by and removed the wrecked vehicle, and we continued our journey.

The nightmare was only beginning. Urged on by the Kashmiri businessmen to make up for lost time, our driver lit up a massive joint and with devilish enthusiasm accelerated round each death-defying hairpin bend. I urged him to slow down but he laughed derisively at the memsahib and went faster. The Kashmiris were enjoying the sport, the Indians were white with anxiety, the Ladakhis were either sleeping or mumbling mantras, and the French cried aloud in terror. Bend after bend up, bend after bend down, all passed in an endless labyrinth. Death lay in wait a few inches away. The sky came closer, the air became thinner, shadows fell on the rock face as the sun set in a peacock display of emerald, turquoise and silver. Night fell, but defying the safety of the curfew, we travelled on. It seemed like the final journey for all of us.

I began to wonder why I went to remote mountain places when I had always experienced a fear of falling. I mentally went through all the steps in the final moments before death. I imagined the terror of being suddenly airborne, falling and then disintegrating with an enormous shock. I contemplated the alternative — getting out and walking in the dark — but I knew with certainty that I would be picked up by the army and anyway, I was truly paralysed with fear. I put my hand on the rucksack, ready to grab the Buddha when the final plunge into darkness came. I tried to make myself ready for death, remembering Shakespearean lines like 'If not now then 'tis to come', I prayed to Tai Situ, I said mantras. I kept my hand on the rucksack. Finally, mercifully, I just blanked out.

Some time later we staggered to a sudden halt in the middle of nowhere, burned out from exhaustion and seeking shelter. We were off the mountain and, though I didn't know it then, a bare four hours on flat road from Leh. The danger was over. It was 10 pm – fourteen hours into the second day of our journey. I clutched the rucksack and stumbled into the night, bright with huge stars. We were at an altitude of 14,000 feet and walking was groundless, unreal. I wondered if I had actually died and this was the *bardo*, so other-worldly and intangible did everything seem. My only reference point was the Buddha statue so my first thought was to see it again. I entered a bare whitewashed room and under the flickering naked light bulb opened the rucksack. I pushed my hand in and pulled up an empty cloth. There was no Buddha! In disbelief I threw everything out ... but no Buddha. I was shattered and immediately my mind raced to work out how it had been stolen. It must have been the Ladakhi behind me who cunningly seized his opportunity, probably when I had blanked out. Or did it happen when we got out of the bus in the afternoon to cross the river? Perhaps someone got on earlier and quickly snatched it. There was no rest in my sleep that night, the ground had been swept from under me.

The next day, under the penetrating stare of a very blue sky, the bus driver stopped, unloaded all the baggage and – according to our pre-arranged plan – informed the passengers that a sacred object had been stolen and I was to be allowed to search their baggage. There was an undercurrent of unrest from the Indian tourists, which grew to shouts and exclamations as I began the search. How dare I accuse them of stealing? The Kashmiri dealers complained about the loss of time, while the Ladakhis continued their mantras unperturbed. After feeling around hastily in two pieces of luggage, I came to terms with the hopelessness of my task and gave in to public opinion. Impermanence, said the Buddha, is the nature of all composite phenomena. What has been brought together, separates. Go with the flow, I said as I resigned myself to the dreadful loss.

I had some wonderful adventures visiting sacred places in Ladakh that summer but none that made me happier than the letter from Tai Situpa on my eventual return to the post office in Srinagar. It was handwritten and altogether natural.

I could not come to Ladakh this summer due to visa problems, but if not happened then would go together and share happy times, why not? When you come back you are welcome to stay at Sherabling as long as you like. It is your home.

It was early autumn when I arrived, breathless with anticipation, at Sherabling. The monsoon had just ended, leaving giant green foliage, fields studded with wild tulips and swirling muddy rivers – a landscape almost unrecognizable from the dusty pine forest screeching with cicadas I remembered in June. Immediately I went to Tai Situ and told him the story of my stolen statue. He listened carefully.

'Stolen?' he said. 'I don't think it was stolen.'

'What happened then?' I asked.

'Oh, I think it went back to its original home.'

'*Dharmakaya?*' I asked dumbfounded.

'Yes. Disappeared.' He searched for the right word. 'Dematerialized,' he said slowly, pronouncing every syllable.

'Is that good . . . or bad?' I was shaken.

'Good, I think good . . . Yes I think very good.'

That was my initiation into sacred empowerment, the blessing power of the buddhas.

PART I

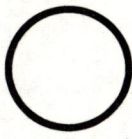

Sacred Objects:

Empowerment, Revelation, Expression

I

○

The Body of the Buddha

It was a flying start, a push through the sticky membrane that binds us to conventional reality into the limitless spaciousness of enlightened mindstream. There was no logical explanation to cling to, but an insight arose spontaneously in my mind – that the empowered Buddha statue had absorbed the negativity of that dangerous and terrifying journey and in the process its materiality was 'used up'. It had saved our lives and become absorbed into the pure realm of origination, the *dharmakaya*. It had gone home.

Recently I received another demonstration of pure buddha nature, and understood that a living person may also manifest *dharmakaya* in this way – in the truth body of a buddha. It was spontaneous perception, beyond the analysis of conceptual mind. Again, it happened in India.

Like so many spiritual journeys mine took place in India, an impossible country charged throughout with grace. Impossible to catch a bus or drive a car, impossible to phone anywhere or communicate, impossible to build a house or grow a garden, drink the water, cash a cheque, use the toilets – and only barely possible to eat anything.

I experienced all these impossibilities during the five years I lived at Tai Situpa's monastery in the remote Himalayan foothills and, with grace, overcame them. At Sherabling I built a house, grew flowers, fell in love and practised meditation. From the balcony of my house there was a clear view of the monastery crowned with its golden stupa, the white-capped jagged Himalayan peaks carved into limitless blue sky behind. Occasionally in winter a leopard would come down from the mountains at night and carry off a small dog or calf. Giant iguanas like miniature dinosaurs sunbathed on the boulders near my front door. I swam in a mountain lake formed by the river where the torrent of water had sculpted a chasm into boulders, leaving a landscape of rock faces and limbs smooth and sensual as reclining nudes; and turning round unexpectedly once, saw the unmistakable hood of a cobra as it flexed its powerful head in the late afternoon summer heat. Nature was charged with a vibrance that I could feel in my cells, sometimes overpoweringly so. As dusk settled into night there was a fearful mysteriousness in the pine forest, alive with invisible entities – human beings were trespassers there. When I stayed in retreat I smelled a very pure fragrance that nothing outside ever matched. Deep within I experienced the gracewaves of the guru's blessing.

The impoverished village woman who carried water for me every day and rubbed cowdung over my floor once a month said to me, in between tugs on her beadie, 'They say that life is *sukkha* [sweetness] and *dukkha* [bitterness], but I've had only *dukkha*.' Her large anxious eyes and cardboard-thin frame taught me compassion and we had no problem communicating. When the awe-inspiring Buddhist master Karmapa, head of the Kagyu sect, passed away in Sikkim, I had sunk every last rupee into my 'dream' house at Sherabling. I went to my local builder's supply shop in the village and said, 'My guruji has just died in Sikkim and I must go there to take blessing from his holy body, but I have no money now for three months.' The shopkeeper's eyes lit up with recognition at the word 'guruji'. 'How much do you need?' he asked.

'One thousand rupees,' I replied, not daring to ask for one rupee more than I really needed. He put his hand in the till, counted out two thousand and wished me safe journey and great blessing.

The outer layer of India is chaotic, hazardous and materially dysfunctional, the land of not-quite-right, where electric plugs start to melt if you use a heater and iron at the same time, where buses overtake lorries on blind corners up treacherously narrow mountain roads, and it is often faster to go to the person you wish to speak to than to phone. But at the heart of India, in the northern centre of the country, under the massive branches of the bodhi tree 2500 years ago, the Buddha became enlightened. The ripple effect of that heroic spiritual achievement vibrates through every human being in India, from deposed maharajahs on ivory chairs rocking on the verandahs of summer palaces in the gardenia-intoxicated evening air, to black-skinned shrivelling lepers, brushing the flies off their rotting faces and limbs. Customs officials, policemen, rickshaw drivers, businessmen, high-ranking army officers, street sweepers – every caste, every religion, every one of the 800 million people born on that impossible subcontinent has a spiritual inheritance like a genetic implant and understands that enlightenment is the end of suffering. Their eyes light up with intuitive recognition when they see a holy person or hear the word 'guru' – master, spiritual teacher. The heart of India is profoundly holy.

So when I entered this mandala, the mindstream born from mastery over thousands of years of esoteric science, it opened a deeper level in my own being and I attracted circumstances that were at times magical. I have an indelible memory of my momentous first encounter with the exiled spiritual king of Bhutan, who was living in Mandi, and of whom I had heard only the previous day. As I approached the tumbledown steps leading to the verandah of the decaying palace, I saw a young man in a suit looking in the mirror adjusting a blue turban-like handkerchief on his head. He turned around with perfect timing as I came up the steps, held out his hand and greeted me, though we had never seen each other before and my visit was totally unplanned. 'It's taken you a long time to get here,' were his first words.

A year later I realized that I had opened Pandora's box. Our relationship was full of obstacles that were far beyond my understanding or power to affect. I was stuck in a palatial rajah-style guesthouse in Delhi in the sweltering pre-monsoon heat waiting for some money to arrive. Penniless, I passed the time by lying on my single bed in the huge dormitory room watching the fan spin and taking cold showers. On the third day a black man entered the room. Before we had said more than a few casual words, he revealed a great knowledge of the relationship and instructed me how to overcome obstacles. I followed his instructions. Everything came to pass as he said – and I have never seen him since.

My experiences, which defied conventional logic, could only have happened in a place like India where the 'cellular structure' is so highly attuned to the spiritual that another dimension of truth spontaneously opens. I was not aware of it then, but I had connected with the deeper meaning of pilgrimage: going to a holy place to absorb and be awakened by its blessing power. It was an auspicious event – unplanned, unsought after, completely unconscious.

On my first overland journey to India I suddenly found myself sitting beside a worn-out traveller in a taxi going down the Khyber Pass that separates Afghanistan and Pakistan. He told me with world-weary conviction that everyone who stays in India is changed by it for ever, and I would be too. I looked at his scruffy clothes, his dirty hands and wasted frame with disdain and decided that I would not be. After all, what was there to change? I was already a Buddhist and my path was very clear.

Nine months later, when I re-emerged, I remembered his words. I would never be the same again. The seed of my inward development had been waiting for the setting where conditions were right for it to grow, just as the seed of a plant will lie dormant till the spring. Everyone who loves India is hooked on that inner level, whether they know it or not. It is the experience of grace, and it is transformative.

The setting for this dimension is vast. The Buddhist view of the world, of time and place, is on a completely different scale from the conventional reality of linear time and solid distinct place. There is no denial of conventional reality, it is just that it is a narrow perspective. Time is actually beginningless because our experience of the world is a mental projection; but as those projections clear we awake from the sleep of ignorance to become buddhas. When did it all begin? The second we veiled our pure buddha nature with a fundamental mistake – the notion of 'I'. So when we fail to recognize self-recognition we call it 'I'. When we fail to recognize our own reflection we call it the object. That is the Buddhist genesis of the world, or *samsara*. There is no need for an historical 'in the beginning'. It is happening every second.

In the real beginning there is only pure buddha nature, and in the end also. In between, we experience the mistake. Like the fairy princess we have pricked our finger on the spinning wheel and fallen into a deep sleep. Bewitched by our own projections we wander in *samsara*, experiencing an endless cycle of birth, old age, sickness and death, leading to rebirth. In the dream of ignorance we experience all the six realms of existence from heavens to hells. Ghosts, animals, humans, gods – all of us on the revolving wheel of life take birth according to the projections we mistakenly create. While in this state of ignorance, there is no exit from the revolving wheel of life. In the Buddhist view there are three kinds of dream: the dream of night-time which ends with daylight; the dream of each life-time which ends with death; and the dream of ignorance (*samsara*, or the world) which ends with enlightenment. The only

The Body of the Buddha

way out is to wake up completely, return to our true nature as it was in the original beginning, before 'I' separated out to create *samsara* and became deeply lost in it — so lost, in fact, that we do not even know that we are lost.

From beginningless time there have been buddhas — beings who have awakened to their ultimate potential. We are inseparable from buddhas — complementary to them like the palm and surface of the hand. High up in a mountain hermitage in Nepal, I requested the great master Tulku Urgyen to point out the nature of mind to me. My third attempt to receive that transmission had a dauntingly precise edge to it as my plane was due to depart in two hours and the clouds were gathering in an electrically pale sky; but the ingredients had assembled neatly at the last moment and I was ready.

We sat opposite each other as the demonstration began. Tulku Urgyen slapped his hand hard on the ground to bring my mind into focus. Then he held it up so that the palm faced outward. 'That is sentient beings,' he said. He revolved his hand slowly so that the palm faced inward. 'This is buddhas.'

It was a non-verbal transmission, a demonstration of the landscape of the mind. We look outward and see external reality as if it were separate from ourselves; buddhas turn it around and see phenomena as a projection of mind. We are buddhas facing the wrong way.

This overview of the psychological origins of the world, or *samsara*, creates a circle, not a straight line. In the evolutionary development view of origins there is a linear progression from a one-celled life form to the refined, sensitized multi-level 'corporation' that we are now. With that goes the underlying idea that we are getting better all the time: living longer, and increasing in height, life-span, knowledge and capability. This is true, but it is the truth of the blind man feeling an elephant's tail and saying, 'truly the elephant is like a snake.' It is accurate as far as it goes, but it does not go far enough.

The Buddhist view pushes out the frontiers of time with a perspective so vast it shatters conventional belief systems and their many underlying assumptions. We are now in the aeon or *kalpa* of the thousand buddhas called the Fortunate Age, because in this particular stretch of endless time one thousand historical buddhas will appear. Sakyamuni Buddha, who appeared 2500 years ago, is the fourth historical Buddha in this particular aeon. When the previous Buddha, Kashyapa, appeared, it seems that people were giants and their life-span was many thousands of years. One Buddhist text, referring to this unchronicled past, describes people at that time as children after 500 years.

'I myself have seen some barley the size of a walnut from the past,' said Tai Situpa when we were discussing this subject. 'I saw one in Palpung [Tibet] in the *yangum*, the quintessence box which was destroyed during the Cultural Revolution. From there they took a few pieces of barley which were smaller than an egg but a little bigger than a walnut. It *is* barley, you can see that. But it doesn't mean that trees will be dwarf trees for them. Everything will be proportionate. This proof [of a past age] doesn't go very well with the scientific description of evolution,' he admitted, 'but there must be links and explanations.'

Indications about the future are precise and well recorded. Sakyamuni Buddha predicted that his teaching would exist for only a certain period of time: the Golden Age of Buddhism when people could get enlightened instantly, would, he said, give way to scholarly debating; then that would degenerate to only the sign or symbol of moral conduct in an outward show of monks' robes. When that symbol of morality passes, the fighting time begins, people will wear weapons as ornaments and there will be a great war between worlds. In the great expanse of time before the next Buddha Maitreya appears, the life-span will decrease to ten years and the human body will be reduced to Lilliputian dimensions. It is recorded that when Maitreya becomes enlightened, the life-span will have increased to 20,000 years.

'How long will it take for this to happen?' I asked Tai Situpa.

'Right now there's about seventy-five years of life,' he calculated, 'and then it will go down to ten years. Every hundred years it will go down by one year. When it gets down to ten years, it will pick up and improve. For every hundred years it will improve by one year. When it has improved up to the standard of 20,000 years, then Lord Maitreya will appear.' According to this method of calculating time, the Maitreyan age is 2,005,500 years into the future. He is the fifth Buddha out of one thousand in this aeon. There are numberless aeons in the past. So we are talking about eternity.

This is the Buddhist view of historical time. When the glue of ego-clinging sticks us to a solid lump of reality, we manipulate it in many different ways. Like Sisyphus pushing the boulder up the hill only to see it roll down again, it is an endless task. There is no limit to the ways of manipulating objects based on the notion of ego, so historical time is endless. For the enlightened mind, there are no boundaries, no time divisions. A Buddha can expand an instant into a kalpa and dissolve a kalpa into an instant. 'Yesterday and one thousand years ago are the same to me, actually,' said Tai Situpa, dismissing historical time.

Cosmology in the Buddhist view is equally vast. To show the infinite places of manifestation, the Buddha Vairochana – who is the perfection of form – sits holding a begging bowl in which there are twenty-five lotuses, corresponding to the different points along the major axis of his body. In every lotus there are millions upon millions of galaxies. On the thirteenth galaxy and the thirteenth group of universes – which corresponds to the heart centre of Vairocana's body – is the 'Universe of Enduring'. One of the planets of that universe is the earth. That is us – enduring the pain and torment of ignorance, aggression and passion. Our particular form of delusion creates the desire realm, and this planet is the stage for our special play.

Into this vast psychodrama, the supreme archetype is born in a form that corresponds to the highest ideals of beauty of the people of that time. The body of the historical Buddha shows the form of ultimate truth and it bears thirty-two major marks of perfection. How does this happen? Through a single-minded accumulation of virtue that is almost inconceivable.

Just before reaching enlightenment, in the fourth watch of the night as he entered into the profound *samadhi* of great love, all the temptations gathered to disrupt Sakyamuni's attainment of buddhahood. He rested his mind in compassion and remained unharmed. When they asked him to explain his power he replied, 'You are not able to harm me because for three countless aeons I have gathered the accumulation of merit and now is the time for the achievement of buddhahood.' He touched his right hand to the ground to call upon the earth to witness his vast karmic storehouse of virtue. The ground shook as the earth goddess appeared, whereupon the temptations acknowledged defeat and disappeared. The last speck of delusion cleared from the glass and the conqueror awoke at dawn into final and complete liberation.

The body of the Buddha is deeply significant because it bears witness to the highest perfection a human being can attain. Every historical buddha, past, present and future – as well as every image or painting made of his form – has to show the thirty-two major marks.

On the palms of his hands and the soles of his feet are the marks of the eight-spoke *dharma* wheel, the perfection of respect for the guru. The palms of his hands are even because he showed the true path to beings, and soft to the touch due to befriending others. The merit of saving lives gives him nails like crystal. His arms reach down to his knees because of his generosity; his ankles are not prominent because of his humility; the calves of his legs are smooth like an antelope because he holds the *dharma* totally. As a result of keeping celibacy his penis is drawn into his body.

His voice has a very beautiful quality because he gave *dharma* teachings. His tongue is long and slender because he spoke only truth and gives a supreme flavour to any taste because he nursed the ill. His teeth are pure because he gave jewels to others, with twenty above and twenty below because he avoided slander; and they are regular because he reunited people who had quarrelled. Owing to the beneficial actions of his body, speech and mind, his eye teeth are long and sharp.

The backs of his hands, his shoulders and the nape of his neck are all especially beautiful because he gave food and drink to others. Because of practising the ten good actions his upper body is very large and wide, especially the upper surface of his hands because he gave medicine and clothes. His body is perfectly proportioned in height and width through the power of resting in meditation. His shoulders are round, the mark of providing refuge from fear.

The lines of his throat are like the pattern of a conch shell, the perfection of giving medicine to the ill. His eyes are very long, like two petals of an utpala flower, the mark of his compassion and love; and his eyebrows are rounded and symmetrical because he eradicated anger. A hair between his brows coils clockwise because he praised beings, and the hairs of his pores similarly turn clockwise because he abandoned worldly activities.

His skin is a golden colour because he gave land and houses, and fine because he was adept in the practice of *dharma*. His cheeks are rounded and full, like the cheeks of a lion because he abandoned empty speech. Through the merit of non-violence the hair on his head is a deep blue colour, like a peacock, with the subtle form of a head-mound or *usnisha*, the mark of great devotion.

The perfection of the four ways of gathering beings around him shows in the web of light connecting his fingers. Through the unceasing practice of good actions, his whole body is surrounded by a halo of light, a supreme aura radiating many feet in all directions. It is said that no one ever saw the top of the Buddha's head, but this is a poetic way of describing the inconceivable. Like the middle of the sun, who could dare to gaze at it?

The physical body of the Buddha is a body of truth which can awaken people from the dream of ignorance. Here is the story of how it happened in the time of the Buddha when collective merit was strong and purity of mind could manifest like a lotus in a clear lake. It is also the history of the origin of Buddhist art.

There was a young princess living in Ceylon called Mutig Trichen, who heard of the Buddha's greatness and developed an overpowering wish to go on a pilgrimage to India to receive his blessing. She begged permission from her parents to make the hazardous journey, but fearing for her safety, they forbade her to leave. In desperation she wrote a letter to the Buddha, communicating her feeling of devotion, her longing to see him and her impossible situation. 'So I beseech you to send me your blessing.' She gave the letter to a pilgrim bound for India.

When the Buddha read her letter he was so moved by her sincerity that he immediately sent for the best artist. Positioning himself at the edge of the ocean so that his reflection shone in the water, he instructed the artist to look at the reflection and make an exact likeness from it. When the painting was completed, the Buddha sent it to the princess. As soon as the princess saw the painting – which was the painting of a reflection – she realized the true nature of all phenomena and became an *arhat*, a person at a lower level of enlightenment.

The princess saw the reflection of the perfection of form with the special features of that perfection and instantly recognized the true nature of phenomena – that it is a reflection, a projection of mind. So the body of the Buddha demonstrates ultimate truth, if we have the purity of mind to see it. In Buddhist terminology, it is called the *nirmanakaya* form of the *dharmakaya* – or the truth body born from the womb of origination. That is why the body of the Buddha has the power to awaken us – it is our inherent perfection.

This truth body can demonstrate ultimate truth in many different ways in response to the needs, capacities and dispositions of different beings. If this sounds slightly remote and theoretical, it is not. My own experience has confirmed it and, like the dematerializing Buddha statue, it is a very personal experience. I share it only to strengthen inspiration and create the conditions for enlightened phenomena to manifest.

Sherabling has a special kind of power for me, a magical charm almost. So enchanting is the natural landscape that surrounds it, so dense and impenetrable on all sides, that I used to become deeply lost trying to find it, as if a magical spell had made it invisible. The Kangra valley in the western Himalayas where it is set, has for thousands of years been home to masters of enlightenment. The renowned yogi Tilopa inhabited a waterfront cave about thirty miles away; and at the other end of the valley the Tantric Buddha Padmasambhava transformed fire into water and left footprints on the rock. So it is a valley long accustomed to miraculous display, and there is a radiance in the air, a sparkle in the water, a lightness like laughter in the elements.

In this setting, Sherabling, as the mandala of Tai Situpa, is an empowered environment where, in the tradition of the great masters of old, the teaching beyond words arises. It can happen anywhere – there is no intentionality in the mind of the buddhas. But the mandala of the guru is the most powerful environment to give birth to genuine devotion.

The inner landscape on this particular occasion was quite ordinary. I had been waiting at Sherabling for three months to complete a project involving Tai Situpa. It had enormous significance for me, so I waited, patiently but expectantly. The whole thing was taking so much longer than I had planned that my money had run out, and my return air ticket and visa had both expired. I felt exhausted and run-down on a daily diet of boiled cabbage, watery lentil soup and turmeric-coated fried potato. It was time to go home.

All of this was routine, fairly bland in fact for my mental and physical endurance threshold. After all, I had built a house with no assistance, no knowledge of local language or habits, design or climate in the jungle of Sherabling – where every monsoon the road is washed out, there is no telephone, the nearest village is five miles away, the water dries up in summer, and both cement and wood are 'hot' black-market commodities. So when it comes to waiting for a great jewel to be placed in my hand, I have no problem eating boiled cabbage and greasy yellow potato for three months.

This time, though, there was a jolting dislocation: the unthinkable was happening. Every attempt I made to see Tai Situpa was somehow neatly blocked, like a game of chess with a master player. He seemed to be inside a protective circle with invisible walls that were keeping me out. It plugged right into my deep-seated fear of abandonment, a fear that throws me into a state of trembling dread and anxiety. What if I couldn't see him? What if he disappeared?

I was holding out quite well in this siege against hope and fear, deeply confident that it could not possibly take much longer and that soon he would send for me. So I went to Delhi and extended my visa and ticket, and returned ready to hold out for another two weeks. One week passed and nothing happened. A kind of nervousness crept in, the hidden face of doubt. I began to feel that something inside would soon snap.

With the countdown at four days, I looked out of the window one morning to see his jeep in the courtyard, and in a flash decided to seize the opportunity to see him when he walked down the stairs to get into it. I walked into the court yard and hovered uncertainly for a few minutes. What if he ignored me? I went into the monastery kitchen and sat down uneasily. There was no comfort there either. Compelled to face my fear, I hurried outside and took up a prominent position at the bottom of the stairs.

I heard his footsteps begin the descent and waited expectantly, fully alert, ready for him to round the corner. His attendant came into view followed by two monks. My eyes were riveted to the empty spot where he should have been. Feeling as if there were a gaping hole in my heart, I turned around abruptly and walked back towards the jeep, in full view of the door where he had to get in. His attendant climbed into the back seat, followed by the two monks. The driver opened his own door, got in, started the engine and the jeep pulled away.

I felt distress and confusion, my mind racing in a barely controlled panic. Where was he? Were they picking him up somewhere else? Were they using his jeep without him? Impossible! I looked through the rear window as the jeep pulled away and saw clearly that his seat was empty.

I turned in anxiety to a monk standing near me. 'Where is Rinpoche?' I asked. 'Why didn't he go?'

The monk stared curiously at me; for a few seconds there was no reply. Then he said in disbelief, 'Didn't you see him? He walked right in front of you!'

'Where was I standing?' I shouted in alarm.

'At the bottom of the stairs,' he said in amazement.

Time seemed to stand still. I felt unable to resume my normal routine. Suddenly there was nothing to do. I went into my room and collapsed exhausted on the bed, a deep kind of weariness seemed to go through my bones into my cells. I stopped thinking, gave up, surrendered to the 'impossible'. In my mind I heard, 'the guru is beyond form', and kept repeating it like a litany. I felt shock-waves, as though I had been blasted out of my mind. There was nothing to do but look directly into reality.

In the late afternoon I went for a quiet, slow walk along the sandy road in the pine forest. In the distance I heard the sound of the jeep as it wound along the long dirt track back to the monastery. I waited quietly by the side of the road while it rolled past me. Looking in the window of the front seat, I saw Tai Situpa and bowed with my hands pressed against my heart in the Indian style of devotional greeting.

The next day he sent for me. At the end of our long interview, I asked quietly, 'Did you see me yesterday when you walked down the stairs?'

'Yes, you turned around and walked away.'

'Because I couldn't see you, you were invisible.'

'I wish I was, I would like to be, but I'm not.'

'You weren't there, you were invisible,' I repeated calmly.

He looked at me carefully. 'It's for *you*. If you tell people, they will think you're crazy.'

'Were you *doing* anything?'

'No.'

'I guess you have to say that.'

'No, I don't have to say that.'

I dropped it. There was nothing to confirm or deny. It was pure display, the teaching beyond words, beyond limitations. That is what the body of the Buddha is for.

II

Images of Ultimate Truth

Of course we live in a relative world of boundaries and divisions. The most important and decisive of these is the body. For that very reason — because it is our strongest reference point — an image of the Buddha is a supreme reference point because it can take us beyond all reference points. The decisive factor in whether it works or not is how we connect with it. Spontaneous devotion rather than intellectual understanding is the connecting link. I knew immediately with my heart what it took years to know through intellect: that the image of the Buddha is a sacred object, the ultimate refuge. Perhaps that is what devotion is — knowing with the heart. In that case, my pilgrimage began many years ago.

It was devotion that inspired the first creation of a three-dimensional Buddha image. A patron of the Buddha, who used to offer him and his entourage the midday meal, had prepared a beautiful throne for the Buddha to sit upon. On the occasions when he was absent the throne was empty. Wishing sincerely to have a representation to place on the throne as an object of devotion, the patron requested the Buddha to have an image made of himself.

There were three images created around this time, all of them by a god called Vishvakarma who came to earth to make his offering. All of them exist still. One is the Buddha at the age of eight years, given, in the course of history, by the Indian king to the Chinese emperor. In the seventh century the first Buddhist King of Tibet, Tsongsten Gampo, married the daughter of the Chinese emperor. One of the main reasons, it is said, was to have this precious image in Tibet, which was then a rough and uncivilized country. So the princess brought the precious statue with her. The enormous blessing power of the Lhasa Jowo, as the sacred image is now called, helped create an auspicious environment for the flowering of Buddhism in Tibet and is the most revered object of pilgrimage there.

The second image is the Buddha at the age of twenty-five, now in Bodh Gaya, the enlightenment seat of all the buddhas and the holiest pilgrimage place in India.

The third precious image is the Buddha at the age of eighty, hidden in the *naga* kingdom deep within the waters of the ocean. *Nagas* takes the form of snakes or dragons and are guardians of sacred treasure – images and special texts – which can be revealed only at the right time. It is said in the Tibetan astrological writings that during the seventh month a certain water planet appears which lines up with the jewel on the Buddha's forehead deep in the ocean. When it conjoins exactly, *amrita* – blessed nectar – flows from the jewel into the ocean.

That is how powerful a representation of the Buddha is. It is not a heathen idol, a graven image, or even a fine piece of sculpture. The *body* of the Buddha is revelation – a demonstration of ultimate truth. So a buddha image is the container for his wisdom power, as important in every detail as an aeroplane's shape in making it fly. Every aspect of the Buddha is a 'design feature', the cumulative karmic construction of an eternity of testing, shaping and moulding to perfection. But however meaningful, it is an empty container until consecrated with authentic presence.

It is called empowerment. The *yeshepa*, the wisdom essence of the Buddha, is directed into the image empowering it. The *yeshepa* is intangible but utterly real. We can call it the essential wisdom being, but in fact there is no way to secularize the word and make it more accessible. It is not energy, power or vibration. We have to integrate the idea culturally because our language has no synonym for it. It is the *essence* of Buddha's realization, and since we can only connect to it through a form, it has to be directed into a suitable representation – the actual form of the Buddha. The presence of that realization quality is the *yeshepa*.

The consecration ceremony bestows presence, like putting the engine into an aeroplane. First the statue is filled with special substances – mantras, relics and the life-stick which is like the spine. Then the image is visualized as 'empty', as having disappeared into its essential nature. From this emptiness it arises purified, as a Buddha. Then the *yeshepa* or authentic wisdom being is invoked and merges with the visualized form of the Buddha which dissolves into the image, filling it with authentic presence. So the process is first purification, then consecration into wisdom-being. To complete the process, through mantra and offerings all the buddhas are invited to remain in the object until the end of *samsara*. This is called *rapne* (literally, best-stay), the power to hold or stay in. What remains are the enlightened aspects of the Buddha's body, speech, mind, quality and activity. If the ceremony is performed by a master who has the ability to invoke the *yeshepa*, it works.

The image is then the Buddha. In reality there is no difference between it and the Buddha, but can we realize this? Realization itself is a process, involving appropriate awareness or veneration. Devotion develops, and when it becomes extremely intense it unlocks the door to wisdom mind. It becomes realization – no separation between the Buddha and oneself. A connection of this kind creates the circumstances for its power to manifest because it creates such a strong movement between perceiver and perceived that duality dissolves. Subject and object dissolve into the mind shared by all: buddha mind. The intrinsic value of devotional energy is immeasurable. It goes right off the scale. 'Miracles' happen.

★ ★ ★

I begin to find the first clues on a trail of sacred history, fresh tracks leading into a past beyond the time-line. The smell of realization is powerful and I follow where it leads, like a pilgrim of a bygone age in quest of the Holy Grail. Sacred objects are secret. As I unite with the experience of their blessing, it magnetizes a mandala where spontaneous encounters arise with the precision timing of the unplanned. I investigate intuitively, letting the flow of devotion in my heart become distilled and purified; staying within the expanding sphere of devotion, the stories unfold.

'I have a Tara picture', Dzongsar Khyentse Rinpoche tells me, 'which on many occasions, Jamyang Khyentse Chokyi Lodro talked to, like a human.' As the recognized incarnation of that great Tibetan master, the picture is part of Rinpoche's spiritual legacy. He reveals it in a very matter of fact way during an interview in London.

'It was painted on the wall in Dzongsar Monastery in Tibet. We took it out and brough it to Bir. It's not that special, just a simple Tara painting. No one special painted it, but it spoke many times to Jamyang Khyentse Chokyi Lodro. Many of his attendants even saw it.'

'What factors are involved with this?' I ask, trying to probe analytically into a sensitive area. Enlightened phenomena are linked inextricably with devotion, and devotion does not yield any secrets in analysis. Genuine devotion is spontaneous, uncontrived, free from artifice – but I am interested in Rinpoche's reply, since he is so logical. He delivers it brilliantly.

'That's completely imagination [projection], I would say. Not in a bad way, of course, in a good way. Everything is imagination. *Everything*... For the good practitioner who has stability of meditation to think that everything is the deity, every sound is mantra, every thought is *dharmakaya*, the statue, in their view, speaks. But if there is someone like me near him, a statue is a statue, like that. It's very personal.'

His explanation resonates, propelling me to uncover the profound meaning beneath the lucid logic. Tantric meditational practice is like alchemy, converting impure conventional projection into pure projections of the refined senses, so that form becomes the deity, sound becomes mantra, and thought evaporates naturally into the spacious expanse of *dharmakaya*. For someone who can *maintain* this pure view, a painting of Tara or a statue of the Buddha is not a two- or three-dimensional object. It is free from limitations, the appearance of pure form. It is not a matter of thinking that it is, not a kind of brain-washing process. It is realization – *knowing* a limitless truth level.

There are many stories of statues that spoke in Tibet – the Lhasa Jowo is one famous one – and even well-documented incidents of statues taking on illnesses like smallpox during epidemics, but as I probe into this area I soon realize that I have to tread carefully. In Tibetan culture *siddhi* or spiritual power is the natural sign of the realization of the emptiness of phenomena cultivated through intense devotion. For us, steeped in materialism, it becomes a peak experience, a 'high' or a 'trip'. Culturally, we are spiritual materialists. Can we understand the expression of phenomena in its true nature, though, and turn it into inspiration?

'In our family there is an image of Tara that actually spoke three times,' Sogyal Rinpoche confides. A modern Cambridge-educated lama, Rinpoche comes from a celebrated and wealthy Tibetan family which possesses many sacred images and special objects. 'When Jamgon Kongtrul the Great was in retreat,' he continues, 'it was the object of his veneration. Tara is believed to have spoken to him and said, "Well done, well done, well done." We also had an image of Sakyamuni Buddha ... which took on smallpox in about the 1950s.'

'How would you explain that these objects have special blessing power?' I ask.

'What it really means,' he replies precisely, 'is that buddhas emanate through images – all images, but only if they are blessed. It has to be filled with holy mantras and relics and then it has to be consecrated ... Then it becomes the object of veneration, the object of practice.'

Devotion is a heart-stirring, spontaneous, spiritual response. Sed Rinpoche, the son of the *siddha* Apo Rinpoche, recalled a powerful childhood memory of his father's devotion. 'When I was eight years old, my father took me to a temple in Karsha – in Hindi it's called Tiloknath – where there is a very special sacred statue of the six-armed Chenresig. My father made a *ganachakra* – a feast offering – there for three days. On the last day we went to this shrine, and my father was praying there very strongly, weeping with devotion. The head monk, who is here now, said, "Look at the statue, it's becoming shiny!" So we all went closer while my father continued to pray. And we saw beads of water coming out from the statue and rolling down it. I saw it myself.'

'Having pure devotion is a form of realization.' Tai Situpa seems washed in gold, his voice has a quality which awakens my heart, turning me right around into my own mind. 'Lots of people try to *learn* how to have devotion,' he continues. 'It is impossible.' We are sitting quietly in his shrine room at Sherabling, sharing a few moments in time. Snatched from the whirling chaos of India, I am home again, momentarily centred. Looking for clues, I start to formulate a question.

'When statues have special qualities, like speaking...'

'Some statues speak, but that is not only the statue itself, it's also the person to whom it speaks, their insight, their realization. It does not speak to everybody. Sometimes the master is doing retreat in front of the statue and the statue gives the master teaching.'

'How can this happen?'

'The *yeshepa* is present. It is a very special thing. One of those statues will transform a whole valley; it will transform a whole state the size of Himachal.'

'There are many of those statues at Rumtek. Does it transform that area?'

'I think so. Lots of good people there. Happiness there, in the air.'

Rumtek is the monastery of the Gyalwa Karmapa, supreme bodhisattva and head of the Kagyud sect of Tibetan Buddhism. It is high in the mountains of Sikkim, in the north-eastern corner of the subcontinent, bordering Nepal and Bhutan. It is a mecca for sacred objects because His Holiness had foreknowledge of the Chinese invasion of Tibet and brought out everything he could. In the monastery alone there are over one thousand Buddha statues, old and new. There is so much sacred treasure in Rumtek that the few objects that can be viewed are like a drop of water in the ocean.

People here are devoted. The sound of prayer music is everywhere: the deep thudding heartbeat of the huge drum, the call of prayer horns that touch a primal vein. Spiralling prayer flags carry mantra into the wind, and there is a sparkle, a quality in the air – happiness. The soft murmur of the mantra, '*Karmapa chenno*' – 'Karmapa know, be with me' – is the heart-song of devotion here. The 16th Karmapa passed away ten years ago and the people of Rumtek await with longing the enthronement of his incarnation, the seventeenth in the lineage.

The old monastery magnetizes me immediately, as it had done the first time I was there. Built 370 years ago by one of the great *dharma* kings of Sikkim, Phuntsok Namgyal, it was used by Karmapa on his arrival from Tibet while the new one was under construction. It is an interesting story of auspicious *tendrel*, the interdependence of causes and conditions that ripens into an event.

The King made a pilgrimage to the great monasteries of Tibet, disguising himself as an ordinary traveller. He was not recognized anywhere and no one greeted him. When he reached Tsurphu, the monastic seat of the Karmapas, he was greeted by a party of monks who invited him to the monastery. To his astonishment, the Karmapa announced him as the King of Sikkim. The King realized immediately that the Karmapa had foreknowledge of his arrival, and prostrated to him, requesting teaching. In the course of his visit there he confided to his guru that he wished to build a monastery in Sikkim. So taking a map of the region, Karmapa selected three sites – one at Rumtek, a second at Ralung and a third at Phodong. He then advised the King to return to Sikkim and await the arrival of his monk, who would deliver instructions for building the monastery. The King returned to Sikkim, and on the pre-arranged date a monk arrived to deliver the instructions of the Karmapa.

The old monastery is situated on a quiet grassy spur of land which ends abruptly in a view of thick dark forest and luminous empty sky. Two massive oxen, its silent guardians, catch the winter sun in an aura of supreme contentment and move their splendid thick necks in agreement as we enter the wooden gates. I have been here before – twice – and both times knew there was something I was not able to see, another room upstairs somewhere. But the gatekeeper was always elsewhere and I was powerless to break through the barrier of language and logistics. It is often the way in sacred places. This time the oxen smile and the gates open.

We climb the stairs, the gatekeeper opens the door and there it is – a very simple wood-panelled room, dark, but somehow the air is fresh. There is a glass case in the centre of the main wall and inside that a very clear, large footprint imprinted in stone as clearly as if it were in mud. I prostrate without speaking and sit quietly with heart open listening to the gatekeeper as he tells the legend which has been passed down for centuries.

'After this monastery was completed there arose many obstacles. Many of the monks were dying because of the various hindrances or charms which had been unleashed by demons and spirits. So because it was difficult for the monks and disciples to practise the teachings, there appeared a manifestation of Guru Rinpoche [Padmasambhava], who came in the aspect of an accomplished yogi, a great sage.

'He conquered the demons and left this footprint, and instructed our monks to keep it in remembrance of himself. He said if this object is kept here, there will be no obstacles and hindrances in the future. Since then it has been kept as an object of devotion. There are no more obstacles, our practice is going very well. We have peace and happiness.'

He turns to a small simple statue of the Buddha wrapped in gold brocade on a shelf above the footprint. 'The 9th Karmapa also sent this statue. There are three main Buddha statues from Karmapa's monastery in Tibet: one is this one here. While in Tibet this statue spoke personally to the Karmapa and others, giving predictions and teachings.

'But since it has been in Sikkim,' he adds softly, 'we are not able to hear anything.'

The room is very quiet, sealed off from time. The statue will stay silent till the right person appears. I touch my head to the glass to take the blessing and walk softly outside into the shimmering sunlight.

Up the road is the new Rumtek monastery on a site offered by the last in the line of rulers or kings of Sikkim in fulfilment of their deep karmic bond with the Karmapas. The site is perfect in terms of the geomancy required for a great temple of the Karmapas: seven streams flow towards it, seven hills face it, there is a mountain range behind, snow ranges in front and a river spiralling downhill in the form of a conch shell.

The line of Karmapa incarnations dating from the twelfth century is a lineage of supreme buddha emanations reaching back in historical time nearly two thousand years to the great Indian *mahasiddha*, Saraha. The activity of the Karmapas has often manifested in the miraculous transformation of matter. There is a set of paintings by the 5th Karmapa, to take one example. 'He put all the paint in his mouth,' said Tai Situpa, 'and spat it on to the canvas, and the whole thing – eleven small *tangkhas* – turned out to be the life story of the Buddha. He put the eyes and ears on it, but the main colour and shape – everything in fact – was already there, naturally.'

As well as being enlightened masters of transformation, the Karmapas – who are also one of the many emanations of the Tantric Buddha Padmasambhava – are Lords of all the Tertons and as such, are the main recipients of *terma* or sacred treasure (see Chapter 4). They have also been gurus to powerful and wealthy rulers, like the emperors of China and kings of Sikkim; to the great founders of other Buddhist sects like Je Tsong Khapa; and to other great lineages – the Tai Situpas, Jamgon Kongtruls, Sharmapas and Gyaltsapas. So for all these reasons, there is a collection of empowered sacred objects at Rumtek which is the spiritual equivalent, and more, of the crown jewels and all the wealth in the Tower of London.

Inside the first of three special rooms which contain the spiritual treasure of the Karmapas, there is a shrine which extends over an entire wall of the room. 'Actually, we are only showing this shrine to those who are *really* students of this lineage,' Jamgon Kongtrul Rinpoche said to me, 'and then only those whom we know.'

About six months before His Holiness passed away in 1981, he asked that the old shrine be removed and replaced with a new one. Everyone at Rumtek worked day and night to prepare it. Three days before he left for Hong Kong the work was completed. Then he consecrated it. 'Since then nobody has opened it,' says Jamgon Kongtrul, 'except for taking out the heart *stupa*.'

I look through the bullet-proof glass at an immaculate solid gold *stupa*, the representation of the mind of the Buddha. The Karmapa's heart is inside. A vivid memory of the cremation scene I had witnessed at the Karmapa's cremation flashes powerfully through my mind. Thousands of people were jamming the stairway of the monastery. In the caterpillar of bodies weaving inch by inch towards the summit, I was finally deposited right beside the huge white *stupa* where the Karmapa's body lay awaiting cremation. It was midday on a bright, utterly cloudless day when the flames first licked the funeral pyre. I looked up and saw something I had never witnessed before or since – a perfect rainbow circling the sun. Hours later, in the afternoon, I watched carefully as Tai Situpa went to the door of the *stupa*, as is the tradition, to make a final offering to his guru. He looked inside the door and motioned quickly to an attendant, who came with a silver spoon and chalice. He picked up something from inside the *stupa* and put it carefully in the silver vessel. It was Karmapa's heart, untouched by the flames.

The memory is almost overwhelming in the shrine room filled with gold-painted statues and jewel-encrusted reliquary boxes. I cannot take it all in, so powerful is this place. I would prefer to sit quietly and look into my mind, tap the flow of inspiration, but Jamgon Kongtrul is my guide and he is speaking.

'I think you know what's inside this box,' he says, pointing to a tall black silk hat box. I nod my head. Karmapa means literally master of all activity, of all karmas. As the incarnation of the compassion deity, Chenresig, Karmapa's essential activity – to liberate all beings – is most profoundly contained in the Black Crown. I have seen the Crown ceremony several times, the most memorable being in a very small room in a Welsh farmhouse some fifteen years ago when I knew nothing about the Karmapa, the Crown, or indeed the *dharma*. But when Karmapa put the Black Crown on his head and the haunting music of the jowling stirred primordial memory, the 'master of activity' seemed to leave the human realm. His eyes gazed unblinking into a depth that could only be imagined. He became awesome.

'I know,' I say to Rinpoche, 'but tell me again'.

'In this box is the Black Crown, but this is only the material crown. The real crown is the wisdom crown which is always on his head. In one of His Holiness's previous life-times he was known as the great yogi Korbache. The buddhas and bodhisattvas appointed him as the Buddha of Activity in this dark age. At the same time all the *dakas* and *dakinis* offered him the Crown, thus crowning him as the Buddha of Activity.

'The Crown is made from the hair of one hundred thousand *dakinis*. Ever since then we describe it as the *rangjung* or self-arising crown. This non-material form of the crown is called *rangnang choepen*, meaning self-luminous crown, or wisdom crown. It's always with him.

'So when the 5th Karmapa went to China, the Chinese emperor, whose name was Yung Lo, saw his wisdom crown. He asked Karmapa what this was and Karmapa explained it. The Emperor felt it was very important for everyone to see it because it represents his buddha activity; so he requested Karmapa to make a material form of exactly what he saw so that it would be beneficial for all sentient beings. So the Emperor made it and asked His Holiness to bless it. Since then many great masters have seen the double crown when His Holiness is wearing the Crown.'

<u>Tendrel</u> is the Tibetan word for interdependent connection. Everything we do and have done is imprinted on our consciousness. But there are certain sacred objects – manifestations of the Buddha, or *tulku* – charged with such blessing that they make an enormously powerful positive imprint on the consciousness. There are six ways of doing it – through each of the five senses and through the synthesis of them all. We become linked with enlightened mindstream, and eventually liberated. The Crown brings the benefit of liberation by seeing.

'The origin of the Crown is the wisdom crown bestowed by the buddhas and bodhisattvas on the Karmapa as the Buddha of Activity for this age,' continues Jamgon Kongtrul, 'and in addition His Holiness is a great bodhisattva, so his aspirations and blessing are such that by seeing it, the Crown can liberate. Especially if we see it during the Crown ceremony, at that time particularly, he is in meditation and his mind is not separate from *dharmakaya*. So if someone can make a connection with it during that time, it really has the power to liberate.'

'What does it really mean,' I ask, 'that it has the power to liberate? Does it mean after some time, or on the spot if you have the karma, or will it ripen one's consciousness more quickly?'

'It's really all these, because in order to liberate you have to have all these conditions. You have to purify your karmas and you also have to develop your merit. Since some of the karmas that one has do not ripen, it takes time and it's a very long process – so seeing the Crown makes it ripen quickly and also makes the good karmas develop faster. Then mainly by this, one's true nature of mind manifests at that moment. It doesn't mean immediately at that very time that one changes one's body. We're not talking about something physical. But if someone can really connect at that time, one is receiving the whole blessing of the lineage, so that you're really...' Rinpoche snaps his fingers and pauses long enough to let the silence make his point.

We spend the rest of the morning journeying through sacred history. There is an exquisite classical Gupta-period Buddha with a golden face and lapis blue powdered hair, which belonged to an ancient Buddhist king of Nepal whose daughter married the first Tibetan king, Tsongsten Gampo (seventh century); a set in rhinoceros horn of five superbly carved statues of the Mahamudra realization lineage, from the primordial Buddha Vajradhara, through the *mahasiddhas* Tilopa and Naropa to the great translator Marpa and his disciple Milarepa, made in the seventeenth century by the 10th Karmapa, an accomplished craftsman from the age of seven; and a pair of intricately carved Buddha statues showing the life story of the Buddha, hand-carved by the Indian *mahasiddha* Nagarjuna from white and blue clay which he brought back from the *naga* kingdom. These precious statues remained in India for nearly one thousand years until the fourteenth century when, on a journey to China, the 4th Karmapa encountered five Indian *saddhus* who passed on their sacred treasure to him.

We stop at a small silver and gold carved relic box containing a very precious image of Guru Padmasambhava, made by himself before leaving Tibet and described as one of his regents or representatives. I strain to see it through the yellow gauze curtain and when I finally catch a glimpse, I am astonished. It looks human, alive, like the photograph of someone I know. Unlike any image I have ever seen, this face has lines of maturity. This fully human being inside a small box moves me so profoundly that the memory even now carries a powerful charge.

'When the Karmapa is eight years old he uses this bell,' says Rinpoche pointing to a five-prong bell and *vajra* set, very small and delicate like that of a child. 'It's a hidden treasure revealed by Pema Lingpa and belongs to the *dakini* Yeshes Tsogyal.' The wife of the second great Buddhist king of Tibet, Trisong Detsen (eighth century), and then the mystic consort and heart disciple of

Padmasambhava, Yeshes Tsogyal was an enlightened woman, a *dakini*, the guardian of all the sacred treasures hidden by Padmasambhava. The bell, which is one of these revealed treasures, is very simple, without pattern or decoration. Shining golden and glowing, it looks like fairy treasure.

As we come to a large gold relic box in a very prominent position on the shrine, Rinpoche introduces 'the most important object in our monastery', the 8th Karmapa statue made from white stone or marble.'

'With the leftover stone he squeezed, like that ... and there is the handprint in the stone. It's written there that whoever sees this is liberated – does not have to go through the lower realms. This is written by the 8th Karmapa himself, Mikyo Dorje.

'The statue was not made by his hand, but appeared spontaneously – *rangjung* – made by his power, his blessings. When he asked if it was a good likeness of himself, the statue replied, "Yes, of course." The face and everything is the 8th Karmapa's face.'

All I can glimpse of the face through the yellow gauze covering the box is the Black Crown. Until the 17th Karmapa takes his seat at Rumtek, Mikyo Dorje is 'absent'.

What I can see very clearly is a flintstone squeezed with a hand imprinted on it as though the substance were soft white dough. 'When the 3rd Karmapa said, "Everything is a projection of mind," then he squeezed the stone and it came out like that.' We pass another small, totally lifelike image heavily gilded and painted, with its mouth open ready to speak. 'This one is the 1st Karmapa which taught the six yogas of Naropa three times.' And inside a large golden relic box, again veiled from view, is an important image of Tara, famous for assisting successive Karmapas to make predictions.

We pass by the rest of the objects on the shrine and enter an inner chamber where the Karmapa gives audience. A large throne covered in gold brocade with the Karmapa's bell and *vajra* sitting on it holds the centre of the room. Covering the walls and arranged clockwise are superb *tangkhas* of the Oral Transmission Lineage of Kagyu masters. I cross through the vibrant coloured beams of sunlight to the far corner where Rinpoche is pointing out a very special *tangkha* of the Indian sage Atisa, made by himself. The oldest *tangkha* in Tibet, it is said to liberate on sight. I look at it intensely, taking in every detail. The *tangkha* is very fine, and uses red and gold colours only. Atisa wears a red *pandita* hat and sits in teaching *mudra* while an attendant holds a parasol over his head. I bend down and touch my head to it, holding it there until my knees ache.

On another side of the room in a glass display case is a pair of crossed swords with two stones on the hilts looking like eyes and an expression making it look like a face. These were the swords of the heroic King Gesar, who won every battle with them. An emanation of Padmasambhava, Gesar ruled his kingdom with exemplary virtue as an enlightened warrior. I gaze transfixed by the swords – they have a legendary quality, the essence of heroic warriorship. Then I understand why they look utterly in their right place in that sanctuary with the golden throne, the Lineage of Transmission and the liberating *tangkha* – the swords of heroic warriorship for the Buddha of Activity.

The door closes on timeless time.

There is more here, much, much more: the hammer Milarepa used to build his countless houses; relics of the previous Buddha; a seed syllable spontaneously arisen from the rib of Mikyo Dorje; a statue of Tara made in ruby belonging to the ancient Buddhist King Indrabhuti II; the turquoise that Damema, the wife of Marpa, gave to Milarepa; a turquoise with a self-arising Green Tara which King Tsongsten Gampo wore around his neck; a statue of the wealth protector Dzamballa which was given directly to the 3rd Karmapa by the earth protector of Tsari in northern Tibet; a *phurba* or ritual dagger presented to the 14th Karmapa by the same protector; the skullcup of the great Indian *siddha* Saraha.

I hold a vivid memory of the Karmapa in the small shrine room in Wales, with skullcup in hand, getting down from his throne, spooning 'nectar' from his skullcup into my cupped hands; in bare feet dancing around each one of us in that same small shrine room in Wales like a crazy yogi drunk on the nectar of liberation.

'Who are you really?' a lama asked the 8th Karmapa when he was five years old. The child laughed and said, 'Sometimes I am Padmasambhava, sometimes I am Saraha, and at other times I am the Karmapa.'

I run down the mountainside under a sharp luminous sky, past wooden huts with red geraniums in milk-tin pots. There's a woman with bright wide-set eyes and wind-reddened cheeks living on a slope below the monastery. She has many companions – all of them goats. Goats come out of her front door, climb on to her roof, perch on the rocks, play in her garden, and nibble the clothes on her washing line. I count up to fifteen and still more appear. I try to take a photo of her with all the goats in the picture, but it is impossible. There is a sharp wind even in the hot sun which whips up from the valley and causes chaos with my hair and the clothes on her line. The goats tumble off the roof, climb up and tumble again. We both laugh and laugh and laugh – looking at each other all the while – till the tears come. '*Karmapa chenno,*' we say at the same instant. Then I click.

III

◯

The Womb of Origination

When sacred images and ritual objects are made by an artist they are called artisan emanations of the Buddha. But they are not always *made* in the conventional sense. Sometimes they are *revealed*, taken out from rock, water, trees or larger images, or even brought by protectors and beings from other realms. Hidden treasure, or *terma*, is the spiritual legacy of Padmasambhava, the Lotus-Born One, commonly known as Guru Rinpoche, a supreme truth embodiment (*nirmanakaya*), who appeared on this planet for about 1400 years – from a few decades after the passing of Sakyamuni Buddha (around 420 BC) to the mid-eighth century AD. To appreciate what *terma* treasure is we have to jump out of conventional reality into the truth dimension of the enlightened ones. For that is where Padmasambhava was conceived.

In his own words:

> Some people believe that I revealed myself upon the pollen bed of a lotus in the Dhanakosa Lake in the country of Orgyen; some believe that I was born Prince of Orgyen; and others believe that I came in the flash of a thunderbolt to the Namchak hilltop: there are many distinct beliefs held by different individuals and peoples, for I have appeared in many forms.
>
> However, twenty-four years after the *parinirvana* of the Buddha Sakyamuni, the Adibuddha of Boundless Light, Amitabha, conceived the thought of Enlightenment in the form of the Great Compassionate One, and from the heart of the Great Compassionate One, I, Padma, the Lotus-Born Guru, was emanated as the syllable HRI.[1]

Rays of light from the seed syllable HRI then formed into a *vajra* and entered a spontaneously arisen lotus flower in Dhanakosa

Lake. Here begins the 'inconceivable' – the miraculous life story of Padmasambhava, born of the union of *vajra* and lotus in the ancient country of Orgyen.

But what kind of birth is this? A *seed* syllable forming into a *vajra*, the male symbol, and entering a lotus, the female symbol? Purer than even a virgin birth, it is creation from enlightened thought, the womb of origination, through the method of pure symbol, the *vajra*. How are we to understand this? I turn to the words of the Guru. 'The actions of the enlightened ones are incomprehensible,' he says in his *terma* biography. 'Who is to define or measure them?'[2]

His emanation, Tai Situpa, says exactly the same when I try to squeeze the Guru's life story into a rationally intelligible framework. 'These things are beyond comprehension; we don't bother to try to understand them. It is *beyond* conventional logic, so better not to try to force it into conventional logic. It's not meant for that.'

Jump the circuit of conventional logic then, and let the testament of the inconceivable awaken a higher dimension of truth. It is meant for *that* – to liberate it. To understand the true nature of the life, teaching and blessing of Padmasambhava, we have to listen for the sound beyond words – the mute sound of one hand clapping, or the meaning beyond concepts. If we listen in this way, with the heart completely open, it becomes revelation. The life story of the Tantric Buddha of our age is incredible. It is the *unadorned* truth, a message from the womb of origination: a display of transformation and a demonstration of seeing phenomena nakedly, *as it is*. So listen with the inner ear and let the truth dimension awaken.

Before passing into Nirvana, the Buddha prophesied that one greater than himself, born from a lotus, would soon become incarnate in a pure body to reveal and establish the Tantric teachings. The reasons for this are that defilements of various emotions – attachment, fear, revulsion – are inherent in the birth process. Everyone born from a womb has some traces of it, even great incarnations. Because Tantrism is a kind of alchemy converting emotions into pristine awareness through the subtle channels of the body, an innately pure physical body is the foundation of realization. So just as the life of Sakyamuni Buddha demonstrates renunciation as the path, the life of Padmasambhava demonstrates primordial purity, naked awareness – the inherent condition of each of us, which has to manifest in the Guru who shows the path to beings.

'I came like falling rain throughout the world in innumerable billions of forms to those who were ready to receive me,' the Guru explains in his biography. 'One of my forms was incarnate as Prince of Orgyen in Jambudvipa, and it was my destiny to govern the country of Orgyen.'[3]

Twenty-four years after Sakyamuni passed into Nirvana, King Indrabodhi of Orgyan (somewhere around the Swat region of present-day Pakistan), found 'a fair rosy-cheeked little boy resembling the Lord Buddha'[4] sitting on the pollen bed of a lotus flower in the middle of Dhanakosa Lake. When the King asked the child his parentage and purpose, the boy replied with these profound words: 'My father is wisdom and my mother is the voidness. My country is the Dharma. I am of no caste and no creed. I am sustained by perplexity; and I am here to destroy lust, anger and ignorance.'[5] Because the King's own son had died, he was convinced that the child was the divine answer to his prayers. So, overwhelmed with joy, he brought the radiant boy to his palace and adopted him as his son and heir.

Prince Pema Gyalpo grew up acquiring superhuman skill and strength. He could shoot an arrow through the eye of a needle with a force so great it could penetrate seven doors of leather and seven doors of iron.[6] With one breath he could run three times around the city; he could lassoo a flying hawk and outswim the fish. He was an accomplished musician, excelled in poetry and philosophy and mastered all the fine arts. When he matured, the King married him to Princess Bhasadhara in order to bind him to a worldly life and thus secure the royal succession.

But Padmasambhava, like Sakyamuni Buddha before him, had no wish to inherit a kingdom or lead the worldly life of a king. Whereas Prince Siddhartha tiptoed out of the palace under the cloak of night, leaving his sleeping wife and child, and lived as a renunciate, Prince Pema Gyalpo performed a seemingly outrageous but skilful deed which would ensure that he could never inherit the kingship: he killed the wife and infant son of an important minister, seeing with naked clarity that the effects of their past negative karma could be ripened in this way. In accordance with the law, he was exiled from the kingdom. Stripped at last of his worldly identity, he entered one of the eight great cremation grounds of India near Bodh Gaya. Meditating in each of these eight powerful places of death, he received teachings from the *dakinis* – embodiments of the enlightened female principle – and became perfect in them.

With this radical beginning to his activity, Padmasambhava showed clearly the characteristics of buddha mind, liberated from every limitation, all dualistic pairs, including good and evil. Buddha mind then is beyond conventional morality, but its spontaneous expression is always compassionate, however it is interpreted by us. How can we know a buddha from a murderer? I was once given a simple but profound guide-line for taking life: 'When you can *give* life,' a lama said, 'you can *take* life.' Mastery over life and death is mastery over the supreme dualistic pair and complete liberation from the wheel of existence itself. The ultimate truth is thus a radical uprooting of all our concepts. That is why the Tantric Buddha had to be in a pure body, born directly from the womb of origination – from the state beyond life and death: to demonstrate pure activity beyond all dualistic boundaries. For outside the imprint of time, there is no conflict – no good, no evil.

In this way Padmasambhava sliced open, with the laser of direct seeing, the heart of the Buddhist moral code and plunged directly into non-duality. This is not the story of Milarepa, the great yogi who repented, purified his evil deeds and *then* became enlightened. This is no rite of passage in the life story of Padmasambhava. This is the story of 'pure from the beginning', the story of the naked mind of the Tantric Buddha, the spontaneously arisen purity of the Lotus-Born One.

The whole universe and all the realms of existence became like an open book to Padmasambhava. His buddha mind absorbed all fields of knowledge as he engaged with beings on all levels of existence. He mastered all 360 languages of the beings of the six realms, including the language of gods and demons, and all fields of knowledge – astrology, logic, medicine and the yogic arts. He learned to extract essences of gold, silver, pearl, iron and lapis lazuli to increase health and produce supernormal powers. From the great artist and sculptor Vishvakarma, who made the first statues of the Buddha, he learned statue-making, engraving and painting, as well as the domestic crafts – boot-making, tailoring and drapery. A begger woman taught him to mould and glaze clay pots. Master craftsman, alchemist, doctor, debater, linguist, Padmasambhava possessed a depth and breadth in exoteric knowledge far surpassing the greatest genius of the European Renaissance.

From Ananda, the heart disciple of the Buddha, he learned the Vinaya teachings – the code of moral discipline – and received ordination into the monastic order. Because he wished to find a teaching which, when applied, would be effective immediately, Padma went to what is described as the highest Buddha heaven to receive teachings of the Great Perfection or Dzogchen from the primordial Buddha. The highest Buddha heaven is not a place, however, but a state of mind, 'the "universal expanse" that cannot be somewhere else because it's everywhere.'[7] Similarly, the primordial Buddha was not someone giving him something, but a facet of the awakened mind. So the teaching was spontaneously revealed to Padmasambhava through the power of his awakened buddha mind.

He held complete mastery over all of phenomenal existence: in various forms he subjugated all demons and evil spirits, subdued the deities of other religions, dominated the lords of death, and brought the nine planets under his dominion. In every realm of existence he taught the liberating truth of *dharma*. Monk, scholar, bodhisattva, Tantric yogi, Dzogchen master of naked awareness – Padmasambhava gained complete mastery of all the paths, used all the skilful means and, in fulfilment of the Buddha's prophecy, surpassed Sakyamuni himself in spiritual power. 'I will plant the banners of the Truth in the ten directions of this world,' declared Padma. 'I am the matchless teacher of all.'[8]

At this point the story comes 'down to earth'. There is a familiar geography and a well-documented history in the spiritual relationship that now unfolds with Princess Mandarava of the Kingdom of Zahor. At the furthest end of the Kangra valley in northern India lies the bustling market town of Mandi in a basin surrounded by hills; and thirty miles or so above it along a winding mountain road is Tso Pema – the lotus lake – a large circle of clear water sunk magically into granite mountains. These places mark the setting for one of the great encounters of Buddhist sacred history. It is an episode that demonstrates liberation through Tantric union, a display in which even the outer elements become transformed.

Princess Mandarava was not an ordinary woman but a buddha, born with the thirty-two special marks of the highest incarnation. She was regarded by all as an incarnate goddess, but when the time came for her to marry, she rejected all forty of her royal suitors, preferring to devote her life to meditation. Scratching her face and pulling out her hair so that no man would desire her, she took vows of celibacy, living as a renunciate in silent retreat with five hundred of her ladies in waiting. Knowing that the time had come to liberate Mandarava, Padmasambhava appeared to her miraculously one day in the form of a beautiful youth sitting in a rainbow. Mandarava was overcome with wonder and joy and invited him into her retreat to teach the *dharma*.

It was not long before the King heard rumours that his daughter had been seduced by a Tantric 'charlatan'. Enraged, he threw Mandarava naked into a deep pit filled with thorns, sentencing her to imprisonment there for twenty-five years. The royal decree for Padma was that he be burned alive at the stake. The story here begins to take on some of the ponderous descriptions of classic martyrdom. Humiliation like that of Christ at the crucifixion preceded Padma's punishment: 'Soldiers took Padma, stripped him naked, spat upon him, assaulted him and stoned him, tied his hands behind his back, placed a rope around his neck, and bound him to a stake at the junction of three roads.'[9] The smoke from his pyre lasted for seven days, hiding the sun and the sky.

But Padma did not stay 'bound to a stake at the junction of three roads', helpless and in duality. In this story there is no suffering and redemption, no death and resurrection, no conflicting opposites. The Tantric yogi who can control the elements within his own body can also master the outer elements – no magic this, but yogic alchemy, transcendence over phenomena and attainment of the ultimate non-dual wisdom. Padmasambhava turned the fire into water, a rainbow-haloed lake with a lotus blossom at the centre, upon which sat an eight-year-old child with shining face covered in drops of moisture. 'My activities are as vast as the sky,' proclaimed Padma to the amazed king. 'I know neither pleasure nor pain. Fire cannot burn this inexhaustible body of bliss.'[10]

The stone pit where Mandarava was thrown is still there in Mandi; and the lake which appeared so miraculously shimmers still, bestowing the soft dew of grace on pilgrims of open heart. Cradled gently between stone mountains, Tso Pema, the lotus lake born from the mud of conflicting emotions, is the radiant witness of transformation.

Spontaneous devotion arose in the King and his subjects, and he gave to Padma both the kingdom and his daughter. After practising various yogas, Mandarava requested teaching in the most esoteric doctrine, kundalini yoga. Sexual union using the subtle channels of the body to produce great bliss is the ultimate alchemical secret and the key to enlightenment in the Tantric path. But it is not to be confused with the expression of lust. Padma is very clear about what it is for: 'I myself am unsullied by desire or lust and such faults as attachment do not exist in me. But a woman is a necessary accoutrement to the secret teachings ... Without such a one, the maturation and liberation practices are obstructed; the result, the achievement of the secret teachings does not occur.'[11]

Nonetheless, it is somewhat heartwarming to know, in this heroic epic of divine and semi-divine beings, that there was enough of the ordinary woman in Mandarava — at least at this stage — to experience attachment to the Guru. After making her request, and merely a few days after Padma had departed to teach the *dharma* elsewhere, Mandarava was overcome by sadness and loneliness. Weeping, she fled from the Zahor palace. At this moment of genuine despair, Padma appeared to her and said — in plain language — 'You cannot control yourself, but you are asking the most advanced teachings from me. Renounce worldliness and centre your mind on *dharma*.'

Padmasambhava and Mandarava then meditated together in the heavenly abodes and in various caves. At Maratika cave in Nepal, remote and high in the Himalayas, they performed the *sadhana* of eternal life. Amitayus, the Buddha of Long Life appeared, placed the urn of boundless life on their heads and offered them the nectar of immortality to drink. As well as possessing power over life and death — immortality — they could now become invisible, or transform their bodily substance into rainbow light.

Miracles continued to manifest in subsequent episodes with Mandarava. When the Guru and his consort returned to Orgyan disguised as beggars, the minister whose wife and son Padma had killed previously, recognized him and plotted revenge. Padma was to be burned alive. As the flames raged, the fire was once again transformed into a lake and in the centre for all to behold were the Guru and Mandarava in spiritual union. The fire of lust and hate was extinguished, melted into the fluid of bliss and emptiness. The entire kingdom became devoted to Padmasambhava and there he remained for thirteen years giving profound esoteric teachings.

At certain points in the story, I stop in amazement and wonder, 'What kind of a body did Padmasambhava actually have?' Enough of a physical body to practise sexual yoga — which is how he gained immortality with Mandarava — and to have many spiritual consorts. In fact, the biography reports, 'every woman whom he met he took to himself in order to purify her spiritually and fit her to become the mother of religiously minded offspring.'[12] His mystic consorts are described as being more numerous than the sesame seeds it would take to fill the walls of a house, coming from all the lands of gods and men, from power centres and cemeteries across the earth. From Asia alone there were 'no less than seventy thousand such fortunate women.'[13]

He wore clothes, ate food, left hand- and footprints on rock, sculpted images of himself in clay and bronze, and even left bits of hair behind. 'One of my friends showed me the hair of Padmasambhava,' Sed Rinpoche told me. 'It was very shiny, like a peacock's feather, blue-black. It didn't look like hair. I wanted to taste it, so I grabbed it and ate it; but it just dissolved, vanished.'

'This is an unchanging, supreme *vajra* body,' the Guru explained to Yeshes Tsogyal, 'not at all like the sick, suffering body of ordinary beings.'[14]

'How would you describe the *vajra* body?' I ask Tai Situpa. 'Is it a real body, a physical body?'

'Guru Rinpoche was not in a real body, like an ordinary person. He was born on a lotus, so what could that be?'

'But he manifested a physical form for people at that time.'

'Yes, always. Always he manifested. Even now he can manifest.'

'And that physical form went through activities and engaged with people on this level, you know?'

'Yes, sure – that's what *nirmanakaya* is for. That *is nirmanakaya*.'

In this way, in the indestructible 'illusion' body – the *nirmanakaya* – Padmasambhava manifested enlightened activity for many hundreds of years. As he travelled to various parts of Asia – to Turkestan, Sikkim, Nepal, Bhutan, Sri Lanka – he dispelled obstacles, subdued demons, gave empowerments to karmically mature beings, and everywhere displayed miraculous powers in any guise suitable for his limitless buddha activity.

This is how the biography describes the various *nirmanakaya* forms of the Guru pervading all of phenomenal existence:

> Sometimes he appeared as a common beggar, sometimes as a boy of eight years, sometimes as lightning or wind, sometimes as a beautiful youth in dalliance with women, sometimes as a beautiful woman in love with men, sometimes as a bird, an animal or insect, sometimes as a physician or rich almsgiver. At other times he became a boat and wind on the sea to rescue men, or water with which to extinguish fire.
>
> He taught the ignorant, awakened the slothful, and dominated jealousy by heroic deeds. To overcome ignorance, anger and lust in mankind, he appeared as the three chief Teachers: Avalokiteshvara, Manjushri and Vajrapani; to overcome arrogance he assumed the body, speech and mind of the Buddha; and to overcome jealousy . . . he transformed himself into the five Dhyani Buddhas.[15]

The Womb of Origination

There was no form he could not take, no aspect of nature he could not influence. Like a bridge over troubled water, the various *nirmanakaya* forms of Padmasambhava appeared in order to relieve suffering and show the path out of it. 'I will manifest without distinction in peaceful and wrathful forms, as fire, water, air, space and rainbows – my vibrations passsing everywhere, my many manifestations leading to bliss,'[16] the Guru promised.

There is no historical chronology to account for the huge leap in time before Padmasambhava again manifested his human form. Over a thousand years after his lotus birth, the immortal Guru appeared in Tibet in the recognizable *vajra* body of great transformation. It was the eighth century, the reign of the second great Buddhist King, Trisong Detsen, and Tibet was ready to become transformed.

It was here at this particular point in time that the Guru laid the foundation for his most important and enduring activity in the human realm: the concealment of *terma* treasure. This bequest to future generations brings his incredible life story into a very grounded and 'tangible' perspective. The background to this unique occasion is both legendary and present. It seems contemporary, perhaps because the Guru is so very much alive still.

The King wished to build a great temple within a strong walled compound at a place near Lhasa to consolidate the *dharma*, from which it could radiate and spread throughout the country. He invited the Abbot of Nalanda University in India, the great scholar Shantarakshita, to help with his various *dharma* projects. But when it came to the construction of the temple – the vital heart in propagating the *dharma* – the great pandit was powerless. The demons and malevolent spirits were so powerful that whatever human work was accomplished by day, they demolished by night. The situation was static, all progress blocked. At this point the Abbot suggested that the Lotus-Born Guru be invited to Tibet, for only his superhuman powers would be strong enough to subdue such demonic forces.

Thus a meeting took place in Tibet of four extraordinary, spiritually gifted and powerful beings, destined to shape the course of Tibetan sacred history – and the course of sacred history for all time, everywhere: the King who was an emanation of the wisdom bodhisattva, Manjushri; his Queen, the Lady Yeshes Tsogyal, a wisdom *dakini* by birth and emanation of the goddess Saraswati; Shantarakshita, the greatest sage in India; and Padmasambhava, the Tantric Buddha.

At his first meeting with the King at the proposed site, Padmasambhava manifested a vision of the temple complex for him to see. It was in the form of a cosmic mandala: four outer sections representing the four continents, each with its two subcontinents; and in the centre, a temple like Mount Meru (the *axis mundi*), with an outer wall surrounding and ornamenting it. The King was impressed; in fact, he was amazed by the scope of the design. So far-reaching was the vision of this mandala, that the King immediately named it Samye Ling – the place of the inconveivable.

The King was in some doubt as to whether it was possible actually to construct such a vision. Padma replied with complete confidence: 'Great King, do not be small-minded! There is no reason we cannot do this. You are the King of all Tibet! You have power over all who possess form, and I have power over all formless gods and spirits. What could be the problem?'[17]

To create the vision of Samye then, Padmasambhava had to subdue all forces subversive to Buddhism – not just in that one area, but throughout the country. Instead of destroying or suppressing these energies, he transformed them into protectors and guardians of the *dharma*, so that they became a creative part of the mandala. Now, whatever the humans did by day, they used their powers to continue by night, so that Samye was completed in record time.

At the consecration of the temple all the beings of the higher realms made offerings: gods, goddesses, *dakinis*, protectors and *nagas*. Lights blazed, music sounded from celestial musicians, flowers rained from the sky; the four stone pillars of the temple, placed in each of the four directions, blazed with fire; and the four copper dogs resting on the pillars guarding the four gates barked. All-healing nectar fell from above.

The signs were enormously auspicious, and indicated that the outer mandala, the container for the most precious secret doctrine of the Vajrayana, was successfully completed. It was exactly like making a golden vessel to hold a powerful elixir. Tibet could now become an empowered sacred kingdom.

The second stage involved Shantarakshita, who became the first Abbot of Samye. With the great Indian translator-scholars, Vimalamitra and Vairochana leading an assembly of renowned interpreters in the great hall at Samye, all the Buddha's teachings were translated from Sanskrit into Tibetan. When this outer level of the inner mandala was complete, it allowed the secret innermost essence to unfold.

The core level of Padmasambhava's activity in Tibet – the

concealment of *terma* treasure – happened as a result of the presence of an extraordinary, highly developed and unique lady, the Queen Yeshes Tsogyal. When Tsogyal was born there were many remarkable signs. The earth trembled, flowers fell from the sky, rainbows appeared, and the little lake near the palace of her parents suddenly increased in size. For this reason, the unusually alert child born with white teeth that coiled like conch shells and long blue-black hair, was named Tsogyal – victorious lake. At the age of ten her beauty attracted the local princes who fought to win her hand. There was so much trouble that at the age of twelve her parents sent her away. After years of suffering suitors she detested, she came to the notice of the great Buddhist king, and he claimed her in marriage. At the age of sixteen, through the kindness of the King, Yeshes Tsogyal was offered to Padmasambhava as his mystic consort, and became the closest of his intimate disciples.

Their activity together was phenomenal. They became true partners, interweaving male and female essence into a pattern of light, like the sun and moon. Together they covered the length and breadth of Tibet meditating in caves, empowering lakes, mountains, temples, rocks – consecrating the whole land, making it harmonious, spiritual. Padmasambhava gave initiation and yogic instruction to hundreds of disciples: on many of his retreats ninety-nine out of a hundred disciples attained the rainbow body. He had twenty-five intimate disciples who were all great yogis, each able to display miraculous powers or *siddhi*.

It was to Tsogyal, however, who had been blessed with a perfect retentive memory, that he passed on his entire knowledge. To his lady he revealed his secret heart treasures, 'truly as if the contents of one vessel had been completely emptied into another, leaving nothing behind.'[18] Tsogyal carried not only the lineage of esoteric teachings from the master; she was also entrusted as the custodian of the *terma* tradition for all time. 'From beginningless time,' Padma told her, 'I have hidden many precious and sacred *dharma* teachings. These are inexhaustible and will continue in the future until *samsara* is completely emptied of beings ... You, my lady, must take pains to procure all my profound treasures...'[19]

What were the treasures that Padma hid? What was it that Tsogyal was entrusted with? Precise mind teachings that can quickly bring blessing and *siddhi*; precious medicinal substances that can unblock the channels of the subtle body; power objects made miraculously from 'sky metal' that can give protection from weapons and heal illness; and specially made images – many of them of the Guru made with his own hand – that can awaken the mind lost in its own labyrinth during the 'dregs of time'. He hid them in rocks, mountains, water, sky, and in the primordial sphere of the minds of the twenty-five heart disciples, to be revealed by their incarnations at a predetermined time in the far future. They were concealed, not like conventional property stored in a vault, but through the enlightened powers of the Guru, to benefit beings of the future. 'I, Padmasambhava,' he testified to Tsogyal, 'exist only for the benefit of beings.'[20]

In fifty-five years Padma's work in Tibet was complete. The *dharma* was established, the land empowered, the secret teachings fully transmitted, the *terma* treasures secured. Tibet was truly a sacred kingdom. In the year AD 864 the Precious Guru departed for the Camara subcontinent to subdue the barbarian hordes which were threatening the humans of this planet. He promised the people of Tibet that he would come to them if they prayed fervently to him, especially on the tenth day of the lunar month. In front of thousands of people who gathered at Mangyul in the northern confines of Tibet, there appeared a blue horse fully saddled, surrounded by rainbow light. Mounting the horse, Padma rode off into the sky and disappeared on the sun-rays, flying to the Copper-Coloured Mountain where he manifested a Palace of Lotus Light. He presides there as King, giving teachings and protecting the people of this world. And, according to the great masters, there he will remain till the end of the universe.[21]

For Yeshes Tsogyal there was a different departure and a final essential teaching. Although she was in essence united with the Guru, she had not yet fully integrated its meaning. Her testimony conveys a devotional energy that is the essence of awakening the Guru within, and the Guru in all phenomena.

'Must there be this meeting and parting?' she lamented. 'Is there no way for friends to remain together? . . . For a time all Tibet was filled with your blessings; now only your footprints remain.'

The Guru's last teaching is profound and simple. 'Listen, auspiciously marked Radiant Blue Light,' he replied, 'many times I have given you oral instructions:

Make the meditation on the Guru Yoga your inseparable friend –
Everything that arises is the pure manifestation of the Teacher.
This is the best teaching:
that meeting and parting do not exist . . .'

He pointed out the truth: 'We are now the same, Tsogyal, not for an instant will we ever really part – only for a little while, only in a relative sense, so be happy!'

But Tsogyal was still in distress, overwhelmed with longing, feeling herself separate from the Guru. She threw herself on the ground, pulling at her hair, scratching her face, beating her body and crying. The voice of the Guru, 'majestic and sonorous' gave a last call, though he could not be seen. This was his second testament. Lights blazed from the sky filling all of space, then darkness fell.

Tsogyal collapsed on to the stones, bleeding and aching, calling out again to the Guru. Before her in space there appeared a ball of light the size of her head – the first of Padma's bequests. She remained inconsolable. Again a ball of light appeared the size of her hand, this time containing a box. It was Padma's second bequest. A light blazed, bright as the sun, then disappeared into darkness, deep as midnight.

Through her tears Tsogyal sang a song to the Guru, vividly describing the absence of his form from the world:

> Now we must look to books for teachings;
> now we can only visualize the Lama;
> now we must use images as his substitute;
> now we must rely on dreams and visions;
> now a grievous time has come!

As she lamented and prayed, though, a light came right in front of her containing a box an inch long, the third and final bequest. Somehow this created a profound confidence in her heart; all insecurities and emotional instability were cleared away. She realized suddenly how meaningless is the concept of being with or apart from the Teacher.[22]

Tsogyal remained in Tibet for 211 years following the instructions of the Guru: to transcribe and reconceal *terma* treasures, to benefit beings who were ready with the profound secret teachings, and to give herself ceaselessly. Her body, purified and transformed through yogic mastery, was a supreme *vajra* body, radiant with the vitality of youth, and looking like that of a beautiful sixteen-year-old girl. On one occasion when seven lustful men were raping her, she seized the opportunity to liberate them. Her Song of the Four Joys instructed them how to explore their desire and fuse it with openness; merging heart and mind with hers, they became liberated. When a leper, his body decomposing, spewing with blood and pus and reeking of decay, asked her to be his woman, she served him. She gave her body to wild animals; she gave clothing to those who were cold; food to the hungry, medicine to the sick, protection to the powerless. 'She gave even her own sense organs where they could be of use.'[23]

When she had benefited innumerable beings in this way, the great queen and yogini took leave of the world of sensation. 'This wild lady has done everything ... has shaken things up far and wide,' she declared. 'I have finished with intrigues, with all the fervent cascades of schemes and deceptions; I will take my winding way into the expanse of the *dharma*.'[24] And she admonished her weeping disciples, 'I have not died, I have not gone anywhere.'[25] Some people saw her body dissolve into light leaving little white pearl-like bones or *ringsel*. In the pure light body she reunited with her buddha consort, the Guru, on the Copper-Coloured Mountain.

This is as far as we can take a story that actually has no end.

* * *

I am at Tso Pema on 24 February 1991. Every year at this time on the tenth day of the New Year, Tso Pema becomes electrified, charged with devotional energy. As thousands of Tibetans, Indians and now even Westerners pour into the area round the lake, the build-up takes its own course. The day before Guru Rinpoche Day, negative energy seems to discharge itself; something eventful happens suddenly, like a fuse blowing all the circuits.

The first time I came here eleven years ago, I had watched, appalled, as a bus sailed over the very last bend on the mountain road and glided into empty space. I had watched it roll down the mountainside. A few people were hurt, no one fatally. It seemed a miracle. That night I had experienced a black, helpless rage and had raced round the lake at midnight screaming through my tears. My emotions were turbulent; there had been no space in which to surrender the things I could not change.

This year a jeep rounds a corner on two wheels at top speed and overturns neatly. The driver and his friend are drunk, neither is hurt. Tso Pema looks like a pure land to me. Small islands of long grass glide windlessly across the lake. As they reach the shore, they are strewn with white offering scarves, the Tibetans' mark of reverence. The air is still, so pure under this blue blanket of sky, I feel charged with energy. A Tibetan man with knee pads and wooden blocks on his hands is prostrating around the lake continuously from early morning till after nightfall. The rhythmic sound of clapping wood echoes off the mountains. His eyes shine with joy, reflecting a light of divine love. As I circle the bright water with thousands of other pilgrims, I chant the mantra of the Guru. Sometimes the mantric sounds seem to hit a tight knot of emotion in my heart – old memories, perhaps.

I cannot remember when it was I became devoted to the Guru. It seems I have been searching for him a long time, following his footprints from rock to cave, trying to track him down. His imprint is so high in the caves above the lake, he must have flown to leave it there. I have called his mantra everywhere, in spacious Himalayan forests at twilight where birds with feather-duster tails sweep the airwaves, and in the murky light of urban undergrounds. My song is the mantra, my dance is with the Precious Guru. 'One need only ask, and Padmasambhava will appear before him,' the Guru promised Yeshes Tsogyal. 'I am never very far away from those with faith; or even far from those without it, though they do not see me.'[26]

I have rushed to Tso Pema for this special day, feeling as though I have an appointment to keep. At the first light of dawn I begin to ascend to the caves where the Guru meditated with Mandarava. Leaving the lake behind, I climb past lazy-limbed buffalo sprawled on sun-baked courtyards outside earthen huts, past streams gurgling into rice fields, up stone, and up again, till there is nothing but boulders below, sky above and huge black-winged birds. At the top lived yogis in caves impregnated with blessing. In the innermost cave chamber where the Guru and Mandarava meditated, there is a huge lifelike image of Padma reaching up fifty feet or more into the darkness. I throw a white scarf on it, with a red rose plucked a few thousand feet below, for Mandarava – and sit calling the Guru.

The tightness shifts, my heart expands, embracing space.

When I leave the cave it is late afternoon and the sky is gathering black patches laced with rays of light. I move swiftly, jumping down the boulder trail, through fields to the lake below. Big heavy drops turn into a torrent and when I reach the lake I am drenched. Unbelievably, the Tibetan man is still prostrating. As I approach, running with head down, he points one wooden blocked hand upwards in a sweeping gesture, and beams at the universe, his face aglow. I look up to see a perfect five-hued arc of rainbow light bestriding the lake. I watch it dissolve as the sound of wooden blocks clapping empty space recede into echo. Embraced by fire, water, air, space and rainbow, I run round the lake, soaked in blessing – united for a moment in the mandala of the Guru.

Padmasambhava, I pay homage to you.

1. *Kutshab* (regent) of Guru Rinpoche in *lima* metal from the *terma* collection of Chokgyur Lingpa. [Courtesy of Ugyen Tobgyal Rinpoche]

3. Dusum Khyenpa (1st Karmapa): the statue which taught the six yogas of Naropa. [Courtesy of Tai Situpa]

2. Stone Buddha in the Sarnath Museum, India, dating from the reign of King Asoka. [Photo by Norma Levine]

4. Two Buddhas made from *naga* clay by Nagarjuna. [Courtesy of Tai Situpa]

5. Footprint in stone of Guru Rinpoche emanation at the old monastery at Rumtek, Sikkim. [Photo by Norma Levine]

6. A bone of the 16th Karmapa from which a buddha has formed spontaneously (*rangjung*). Sacred relic at Tsurphu Monastery, Tibet. [Photo by Ward Holmes]

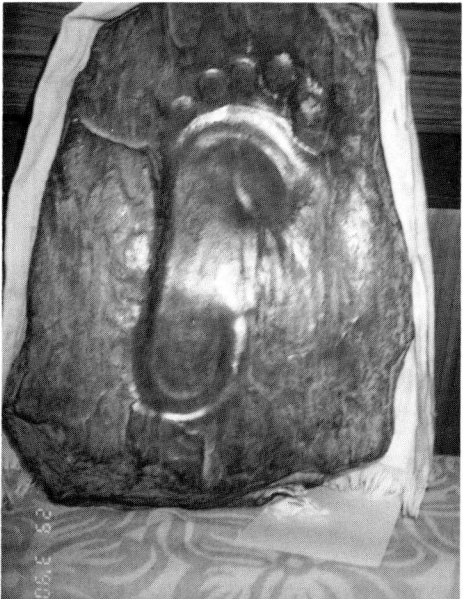

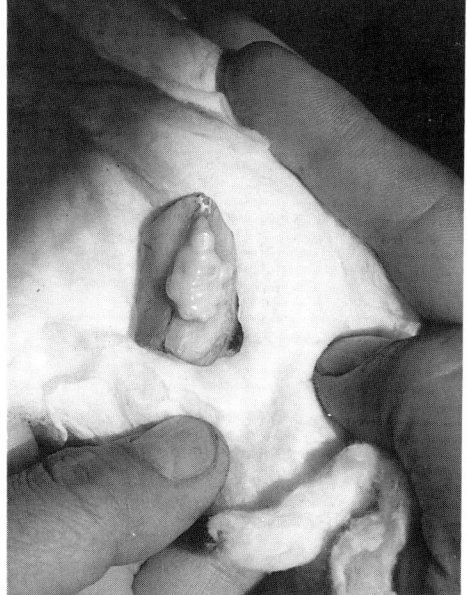

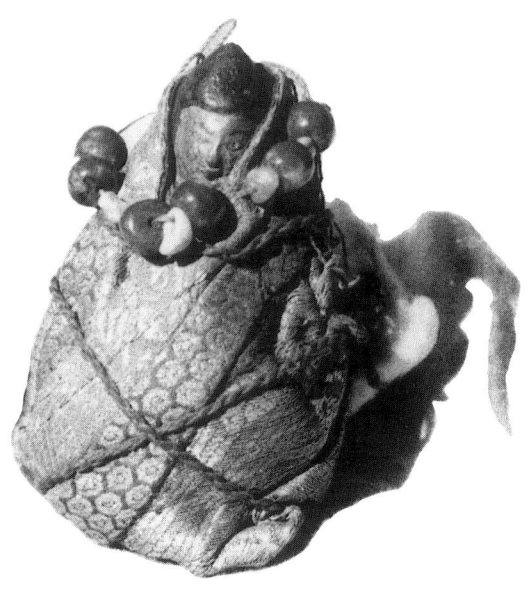

7. One of the five principal *kutshabs* (regent) of Guru Rinpoche. [Courtesy of Tai Situpa]

8. Clay *khutshab* (regent) of Guru Rinpoche with his two consorts, Mandarava and Yesheh Tsogyal; from the *terma* collection of Chokgyur Lingpa. [Courtesy of Ugyen Tobgyal Rinpoche]

10. *Above*: *Namchak* (sky metal) *phurba*; from the *terma* collection of Chokgyur Lingpa. [Courtesy of Ugyen Tobgyal Rinpoche]

9. *Left*: Bell and *dorje* belonging to King Trisong Detsen (eighth century); from the *terma* collection of Chokgyur Lingpa. [Courtesy of Ugyen Tobgyal Rinpoche]

11. *Below*: *Namchak* (sky metal) *dorje*; from the *terma* collection of Chokgyur Lingpa. [Courtesy of Ugyen Tobgyal Rinpoche]

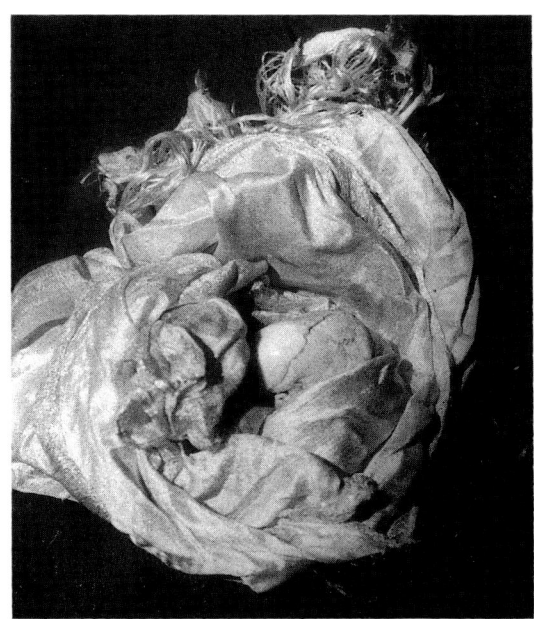

12. Egg-shaped relic of the Buddha. [Courtesy of Tai Situpa]

13. *Rangjung* Green Tara at Asura Cave, Nepal. [Photo by Norma Levine]

14. Handprint in stone of Guru Rinpoche, outside Asura Cave, Nepal. [Photo by Norma Levine]

15. Baudhanath Stupa, Nepal. [Photo by Norma Levine]

16. The inner hidden land of Tashiding in Sikkim. [Photo by Norma Levine]

17. Khechuperi: sacred lake formed spontaneously in Sikkim. [Photo by Norma Levine]

IV

The Limitless Expanse

A long time ago on a bleak winter's day in Wales, I closed my door firmly and set off suddenly for northern Scotland to visit an old friend I had not seen since university days. I knew it would be too long a journey to travel in one day, and since I had heard about a Buddhist centre about half way, I was prepared to spend the night at Samye Ling. I knew nothing about Buddhism, had never even read a book – it was just a convenient place to stop for the night. Late in the afternoon I pulled up at a call-box to phone my friend and tell him I would be there the next day. To my surprise he advised me to wait a few days – there had been an unexpected change in his plans.

Since there was no hurry to get anywhere any more, I made myself comfortable and had a good look around the sprawling, slightly ramshackle buildings of the Buddhist centre nestling near the Esk river in the remote barren hills of the Scottish border. From the moment I stepped into the shrine room, it was like opening a door on to another world. There was the smell of inspiration, sounds that stirred primordial consciousness – the recognition of something that had been lost a long, long time ago. I sat down, riveted, taking it all in, soaking it up like a person immersing in water after wandering for years in the desert.

Day after day I sat there spellbound, watching the great Lama, Dilgo Khyentse Rinpoche, who had just arrived from Bhutan – his first time ever in the West – perform the ritual ceremonies in preparation for the New Year. His presence was vast, the dimension he dwelled in limitless. My everyday mind dropped into it, sinking comfortably like a wave coming to rest in the great ocean.

Later I learned he was a great *terton* with a spiritual ancestry that fused him completely with Padmasambhava.

I took refuge in the dimension I had glimpsed, right there on the spot. Wordless, limitless, deep, a truth dimension that, of all forms of art, only the timeless sounds of Indian flute music have ever been able to approach. Words can only lie because they form conceptual thought, and this dimension is outside anything created. Only being in the presence of one who embodies it can ever reveal it. It was like finding my real self, one I did not know had even been lost.

I stayed there for two months that winter. To this day I have never seen northern Scotland, never visited that friend. There was no need to go anywhere. Quite unexpectedly, out of the blue, in the raw month of February, I had come home.

Padmasambhava concealed *terma* treasure in this truth dimension, the limitless expanse of enlightened mind beyond boundaries. I tried to analyse it, to research how far I could follow the process with conventional concepts of time, place and substance. But I came to an abrupt impasse. The exchange with Tai Situpa was like hitting my head against a brick wall that was not actually there – an illuminating experience in itself.

'When Padmasambhava concealed *terma* in rocks and water,' I began, 'it seems as though it wasn't through ordinary means. He didn't hide it the way you bury treasure and then go and dig it up.'

'Not exactly,' he replied. 'He *concealed* it; then he had particular protectors take care of it, and so on. For example, there's one *terma*, a statue of Vajrapani, which was revealed when one great master asked his attendant to go to a particular waterfall and to bring forth whatever he found. When he arrived, he found a huge sea monster which opened its mouth. Inside was a small box. He grabbed the box and returned.'

'But this kind of thing is extraordinary, beyond conventional boundaries of time and place,' I protested. 'It's not like the ordinary . . .'

'It's not just anybody, Mr Ali Baba, not like that. But I cannot say it's beyond conventional time and space because time is always the same, conventional or unconventional. There are not two different ones. But the reason for concealment isn't conventional. Guru Rinpoche didn't conceal it just to hide it from other people; but when the right time comes, then the right activity will unfold to reveal it.'

'For example, this water monster who's holding the treasure box,' I persisted, 'what kind of existence does it have?'

'It's not an animal in whose mouth he put it. It's a protector. He concealed the treasure and then he appointed a protector to take care of it. Then that protector gives it when it's ready. That animal, that monster, is the protector.'

'But in the time between when the object is concealed and when it's revealed, the solid object, the statue or whatever, is it *there*?' My investigation is relentless.

'Of course, it has to be there, but it's not there like somebody's money is sitting in the bank. Even if you have infra-red machines and look through all the rocks to see the *termas*, you cannot.'

'That's what I mean, it's outside conventional reality.'

'Of course,' he replied with great patience. 'It's just *there*, you know? Neurotic mind,' he said pointedly, 'can never understand these things. There's no point in even trying. It happens, and it's true, and that's how it happened.'

'So is it another dimension of perception?'

'I would not say perception. Another level of truth, of course. These things that we worship, the *terma* and all of them, they have *blessing* power. *That's* the different level, different from anything else.'

Grasping rigid definitions of time and space, compressing solid chunks of matter into the three dimensions of time, does not go together with *terma*. They are there to explode boundaries, to manifest enlightened presence: the body, speech and mind of the Buddha. They are messengers from the truth level beyond boundaries. Like keys to the door, they have the power to unlock the mind to its true changeless nature. That's the blessing they bring, 'the different level, different from anything else'.

It was with his special twenty-five disciples that Padmasambhava established a unique method of transmission, one that would ensure infallible concealment, authentic continuity and appropriate revelation. He joined his enlightened mind with theirs, and with the full power of his concentration, concealed the teachings in the essential nature of their minds – the expanse of the unchanging awareness state. According to an authoritative text on *terma*, the process is similar to consecrating an image, but the *yeshepa* or wisdom deity is stabilized in the essence of the heart of a disciple.[1] This empowerment, unique to the terma tradition, is known as the mind-mandate transmission.

The Guru then pronounced a prophetic authorization, empowering that same disciple to reincarnate at a particular time and place to discover the *terma*. More than a wish, more infallible than prophesy, the aspirational empowerment of Padmasambhava meant that the disciple *would* reincarnate and circumstances *would* unfold to allow revelation. The Guru's words had the power to shape reality.

Then Yeshes Tsogyal devised a symbolic secret script and wrote the code on 'palm leaves, and on blue (or lacquered) paper, in ink of gold, silver, copper, iron and malachite' and enclosed it in various kinds of containers: 'gold-lined boxes, earthen pots, stone receptacles, skulls and precious stones'.[2] The symbolic scripts, known as *chokser*, are the key to awaken the mind of the *terton* — the discoverer of the *terma* — to the complete teaching hidden in his or her essential nature in the ancient time. *Termas* of this kind which rely on the symbolic key are called earth or substance *termas* (*sater*) to distinguish them from 'mind treasure' (*gongter*) which arise in the mind of the *terton* independent of the written code.

Sacred images and miraculously made objects, like *vajra* and *phurba*, were sometimes enclosed with the secret script to amplify the blessing power of the teaching and ensure that the scripts were properly decoded. The caskets were sealed, then hidden in rocks, trees, mountains, temples, images, lakes, water and sky through Padmasambhava's miraculous power. After he left this realm, Yeshes Tsogyal continued the Guru's work and concealed his treasures in all the designated places in Tibet, Kham (eastern Tibet) and Bhutan.

Each *terma* was entrusted to a particular protector to guard and hand over to the *terton* at the right time. *Terma* protectors are powerful 'elemental' beings, living in rocks, water, sky, trees and mountains, some of whom Padma tamed and transformed, some of whom are wisdom protectors — faithful guardians of the *dharma*. The protectors ensure that the treasure is not destroyed by the elements, that it remains safely in its place till the time of discovery — or that it is moved elsewhere if the original concealment spot is being destroyed. They also have the power to grant invisibility, so that no one may take the treasure before the hour appointed for its discovery.

'About one and a half day's walk from my monastery in Kham,' recalled Terton Zilnon Lingpa, 'there is a particular *terma* rock which I have some power to see into. I like looking inside it.'

Zilnon Lingpa is the incarnation of Khechung Lotsa, one of the special twenty-five desciples. From the first time we met, I had a sense of recognition; there was a quality or presence in him which was quite unmistakable. I have come across it before. It is earthy, warm, direct, playful, intimate and spacious – the 'smell' of the Guru. Padmasambhava always seems to come through in that way, strong and clear.

We sat comfortably one clear October afternoon beside the log fire in my sitting room in Wales as he continued his reflections. Spellbound, I listened as he stepped familiarly through conventional boundaries. 'Inside that rock, it's similar to a good housekeeper who keeps articles in a cupboard. Just like that, there are many things inside it, many clothes – Guru Padmasambhava's, Vairotsana's, Vimalamitra's.' He paused a moment reflecting. 'But there's one crystal *stupa* there which I like.' His eyes glowed with delight. 'It's very shiny. Once I tried to take it out, but it broke when I touched it. It's not my share.' His eyes were playful as he made his confession; then he explained in serious tones. 'Without Yeshes Tsogyal's order, the *dharma* protectors will not give it, and also I will not take it.'

He was reminiscing so naturally in this boundaryless expanse, that I asked a natural, analytical question: 'If somebody else was there, some ordinary person, could they also see these things?'

The spell was broken. 'No,' he replied impatiently. Turning on the television, he flipped through all the channels till he found his favourite programme. His eyes glowed again for a moment, then reposed in equanimity like stars settling into the vast expanse of space. For the *terton*, there is no boundary. Everywhere is home.

During the next year and a half, there were many revelations from Zilnon Lingpa. His lifestyle was itinerant, completely spontaneous, and he would just turn up suddenly, enriching my life for a few days with his boundless good humour and warmth. He lived humbly without possessions, without even a retinue of attendants. The precision timing involved in the revelation of *terma* requires a moment-by-moment readiness, and the main preparation for this is to abandon the complications of a worldly life. 'Kings, persons of worldly fortune, laymen, and those attached to property, will not have this power,' Padmasambhava warned.[3]

If the *terton* lives simply, if his conduct is appropriate and behaviour spontaneous, it creates the right atmosphere, and this attracts the circumstances for revelation to unfold. When the time is right, a simple cowherd, who may be totally illiterate, will suddenly be able to read the *chokser*, the 'yellow scroll' written in the secret sign language of the *dakinis* – and even write whole volumes from it. 'Gya Zhangton didn't know any language, not even Tibetan,' Zilnon Lingpa told me one day, 'but I saw his handwriting, and he had perfect grammar and wrote two volumes. Apart from this, he didn't know anything.'

He continued with his story, one of many I was to discover about the wonderful spontaneous behaviour of *tertons*. 'In his previous life-time, he was the incarnation of Sangye Yeshe [one of the special twenty-five]. He just stayed around his house, had a few cows and took them to graze on the mountain pastures. But sometimes he took *ters* from stones. Then he would recount the teaching aloud while someone wrote it all down. Sometimes he gave initiations to his disciples. But if you showed him another text, or even his own text, he couldn't read it. He was totally uneducated.'

Miracles happen naturally when *terma* are revealed; relative circumstances become flexible, bending within the enlightened mandala of the Guru. And it is not ancient history; it is here and now, the present – fresh and vivid. Zilnon Lingpa described an event that happened in Tibet in 1990. Sera Khandro, a female *terton*, let it be known that on a certain day she would reveal some important *termas*. A public gathering of around three hundred people – including several highly respected lamas – witnessed her fly up the mountain to a huge rock and extract from it some images, *phurbas* and other objects. 'I know this rock,' he commented, 'and it's not possible to walk there, only to fly.'

I have read some of the life stories of *tertons*, and their display of miracles from very early childhood is a constant feature. One of my favourites is of Ngedon Drubpey Dorje, a descendant of the family line of Chokgyur Lingpa, one of the great *tertons* of the previous century. As a child Drubpey Dorje was extremely naughty, refusing to listen to anyone or study anything. When his tutor locked him in a room, he could still be seen playing outside; he would hang his clothes on sunbeams. To escape punishment he jumped off a three-story building and then bounced up again like a yoyo when his tutor ran down to catch him. But when he was older, he knew everything without being taught.[4]

One day, after we had completed a feast offering ritual to Padmasambhava and were enjoying the *tsok* (food offerings), I requested Zilnon Lingpa to tell me some stories from his own youthful days. 'When I was three years old,' he began, 'I used to go with my uncle to the Nyi River, where Nuden Dorje's[5] house is situated. There was a cherry tree there, the only one in East Tibet, and I was very fond of its fruit. But one time my uncle refused to take me because the water was very high and he was worried the "mad" river would come and carry me off. So I became very angry and taking a stone, put pressure on it to grind it into the ground. My footprint remained on the stone. A few years later I looked inside the house of Nuden Dorje, and saw that he had also left a footprint there in stone.

'When I was ten years old, I threw out a kettle from my monastery. It landed about half a kilometre away, unbroken. I was also able to prophesy many things and whatever I said came true.

'At the age of nineteen, when I left my monastery, a very large black raven came with me. It accompanied me from East Tibet to Lhasa, and from Lhasa to Nepal. Wherever I went, that Mahakala bird followed. When I returned to my monastery in 1985, this raven also returned there with me.

'It's our belief that Mahakala [the foremost wisdom protector] stays close by the very high lamas of our monastery,' he explained quietly, and added, 'sometimes people see a black man accompanying us. That black man is also Mahakala.'

Closely guarded by the protectors, the impeccability of the *terton* allows a series of precisely linked events to unfold, and the precious treasures are revealed exactly at the right time. This series of precision-timed events is called auspicious interdependence. It is like a perfect chain of pure gold. The support or consort, the time, the place, the materials – all have to line up in an unerring sequence, or the *terma* may be impossible to uncover. The perfect scenario gives birth to the treasure, and they 'enter' our world. The stories of *terma* revelation are thrilling; proof of the power of the Guru's promise.

Sometimes *terma* revelation resembles an incredible adventure story, as dramatic as anything a film director could devise. One day when Terton Chokgyur Lingpa was having tea in a small temple, unbeknown to everyone present Yeshes Tsogyal appeared to him and gave him the prediction of a water monster holding a yellow parchment scroll between its teeth. Its mouth would close at noon and the *ter* would be impossible to take for another sixty years.

Chokling sprang off the throne, leapt down the stairs followed by his attendant, and jumped on to his horse, which seemed to know what was happening because he had already turned around and started to go. His attendant grabbed a knife and cut the rope holding the horse, and they raced off in the direction of a very big river. It was summer and the water level was particularly high. Chokling rode straight into the river and in midstream disappeared under the water. After five minutes he emerged on the other side with the treasure.[6]

I asked Zilnon Lingpa to tell me about his first discovery of treasure. It is rare that these stories are revealed during the lifetime of the *terton* because it can cause obstacles to arise. Perhaps the circumstances and time and place were right; perhaps he trusted my devotion to the Guru; perhaps there was an auspicious connection between us. Whatever it was, he opened his heart to reveal more and more.

'At the age of nine, I was doing retreat in Tibet, when I had a vision. In the vision I was told to go the next day to a certain rock where I would get the *ter*. I followed the instructions and the next day withdrew from the rock a stone with some paper inside it, containing the teachings of Yamantaka. It all happened exactly as indicated in the vision.'

Then he told me the extraordinary story of a *vajra* belonging to Padmasambhava, which had been one of the precious treasures of his previous incarnation Nuden Dorje. This *vajra* was so important, so powerful, that it was 'reclaimed' by the protector when Nuden Dorje died: it was too powerful for any of his disciples to keep.

He continued the story. 'Then when I was ten years old, I was doing the Dorje Trollo ritual, and I needed this *vajra* so the ritual would work properly. During the invocation of Dorje Trollo, suddenly it just appeared on my *puja* table. It just manifested where it had not been before. The *dharma* protector returned it to me, according to Yeshes Tsogyal's order.' He paused and added, 'But when I die, I don't know where it will go.'

He began to reveal more and more of his experiences, the wondrous stories of *terma* revelation. 'On another occasion, I was doing a *puja* with His Holiness Dudjom Rinpoche in front of the king's palace in Mandi, where there are some very big rocks. Suddenly a stone fell into my hand. I thought to give it to His Holiness, who is also Khechung Lotsar's incarnation, but he told me to keep it. So I broke the stone and inside it found a paper with the writing of Khechung Lotsar. Since I'm his incarnation, when I read it I can remember everything from my previous lifetime – when I wrote it, how I wrote it – everything. From this small key I can recall the whole text. Then I wrote it down in detail.'

'I never *try* to find *terma*,' he commented. 'If I get some, that's okay; and if I don't get any, it's okay. Some people think that if they find *ters* they will become famous, and these people have difficulties. I never have any obstacle with finding *terma*. This last time when I went to Tibet [1990], I found two *ters*.'

A telephone rang. There was the sound of passing cars outside the window. I remembered suddenly that we were in the front room of a small ground-floor flat in London. I felt a sudden jolt – like culture shock. It was such an improbable setting for so important a revelation.

'This year, on the tenth day of the fourth Tibetan month [June], I was at my monastery at Khordong watching some lama dancing. During the dance of Guru Sengye [a wrathful manifestation of Guru Rinpoche], the *dharma* protector came.

'There was a strong gust of wind and two stones fell into my hand. One was a Mahakala stone, which was black and white; the other was maroon-coloured and very shining. Inside was a small paper with the key to the Heruka *sadhanas* and *tantras*; and inside that text was the Mahakala *sadhana* and some other texts. The little paper and the stone are at my place in Siliguri, but I haven't written it yet.

'Then on the thirteenth day of the Tibetan fourth month,' he continued, 'I received the last *terma* so far in this life-time. I was at Dongri Mountain, a place belonging to Mahakala, with my son Ugyen and some coolies. I sent everyone to look and see if we could continue by jeep as the road was very bad. In the midst of all this, when I was alone, two *dharma* protectors appeared. One held a stone, the other held a statue of two-armed Mahakala, about five inches in height and made of metal, with a very large *phurba* in his right hand and a *kapala* in his left.

' "Which do you need?" he asked me. "This time you do not have a consort with you, so you cannot have both."

' "The stone is what I need," I replied. "The statue I do not need." I was thinking that the statue would only be of limited benefit, perhaps only in the place where it would be kept; but the stone contained a text which I could write down and then everyone would benefit from it. So I took the stone and the statue was taken back.'

'So when you say you put it back,' I asked, trying to get a clear picture of this extraordinary transaction, 'it means...?'

'I didn't put it back. They *took* it back.'

'The protectors *took* it back?'

'Yes.'

'So it means it disappeared, is that what happened?'

'"You don't have a consort with you this time, so which one do you need?" Then I said, "this stone I need." Immediately they took away the statue.'

'So were you actually talking to the protectors?'

'Yes.'

'Did this happen in a vision, or did you actually see somebody?'

'I saw them.'

'Did they appear as people? Did they have the human form?'

'Human form.'

'Can you say what they looked like?'

There was a hushed silence in the room. Gudrun, his companion, and I both looked at him intently, awed by the detailed description he had given. 'The protectors were looking like Khampa laymen, dressed in Khampa laymen's clothes,' he replied casually.

His familiarity again prompted the obvious question: 'Did other people see them as well, or only you?'

His reply was immediate and rather sharp. 'If everybody sees them, then everybody is a *terton*.' He paused to reflect, then added quietly, 'But I think perhaps Ugyen, my son, saw them, because when he returned he asked, "Who's this?" But as soon as his coolie came back, they disappeared.'

It took me some time to understand the significance of the consort in the sequence he was describing. Through further questions it became clear that had there been the right companion, *both termas* could have been taken. But in the circumstances, it was possible to take only one. The consort or companion is the person who has made the specific wish to be the support for that particular discovery when the *terma* was concealed. For these kinds of earth *termas*, the consort is not always essential.

For the mind *termas*, though, a consort is the most important link, without whom revelation is impossible. The union of male and female energy is essential to generate the heat which will unlock the primordial sphere in which these *termas* were concealed. 'Female energy gives the male more power and heat,' Zilnon Lingpa explained. 'Some *tertons* do not have full power, so they need to use some from the woman.' For this reason, male and female *tertons* alike are almost always married.

The implications of interdependence are vast, and contemplating it can be a mind-expanding experience. Beru Khyentse Rinpoche told me about a 'support' which was an object belonging to the consort. 'When Mingyur Dorje found his consort,' he said, 'she couldn't speak; she was dumb. So whenever he wrote the *terma*, he needed her ring. When he put on her ring, he could write; but without this consort connection, he could not write.' Because the consort had an obstacle in communicating herself, the *terton* needed a support for writing. Her ring became the auspicious link to unlock his inspirational power.

One by one, in perfect order, the pieces fit and the treasure is brought out. It is said that the precious earth *termas* have the power to fulfil wishes: their very entry into the relative world, through the chain of golden links, is due to the enlightened wish that those who can connect with them be liberated.

They are our spiritual inheritance, dedicated to us, the people of the dark age. We have to find and claim them, though. The path to their discovery, as I found out, is through the heart. Devotion to the Precious Guru is the key to the door.

As this understanding of their meaning permeates my being, it becomes an inner pilgrimage for me. The more I find out about these treasures, the deeper I go inside myself: and the deeper I go, the more I find out. The Guru concealed images, *vajras* and *phurbas*. As I research, I begin to find out the true nature of these miraculous objects, and as I absorb the truth, more clues come my way, leading to a personal discovery.

'For the people who did not meet me,' Padmasambhava explained, 'the images will be the lamp for dispelling their darkness.' There were five particular images that Padmasambhava made of himself and empowered as his regent, his representative. He blessed these in a specially powerful way. One text describes it.

In the state of meditative absorption, the Guru commanded the *dakinis* to bring various substances: gems of the god and *naga* realms; gold and sand from Manasrowar Lake, the sacred lake in western Tibet; fragrant wood, medicinal essences, nectar water and sacred substances of accomplishment. 'With these materials and chemical water, [the Guru] made the clay and [then the images] with his own hand, the size of his thumb.'[7] Inside it he put relics of some of the great Indian enlightened masters and his own blood, hair and essence, as well as medicinal substances and ambrosia. At the point where he sealed it up, he painted natural vermilion and protective colour.

Then he performed the consecration. No need to invoke the *yeshepa*: 'The actual body of the Guru melted into a body of light and dissolved for a while into the heart of the image.'[8] Then he emerged from the image and blessed it again.

No wonder it is said by the great *terton* Dodrupchen Rinpoche, that 'if one sees the image, it will be the same as seeing Guru Rinpoche himself; if one makes offerings, pays homage and makes aspirations before the image, that will be as effective as performing these actions in front of Guru Rinpoche.'[9]

The images *are* the Guru, and as well as being most sacred objects of devotion, they have certain kinds of specific powers: the *dharma* will continue and flourish in the places where they remain; they will repair the earth's energy and prevent wars and harmful spirits. The very substance from which they are made is so powerfully transformative that they produce a constant stream of blessed nectar (*dutsi*). One that I have seen has produced a trunkful of this substance in tiny pill form since the time of its revelation. Another that I had the great blessing to inspect closely, and even touch, was black, shaped like a drop, and sealed with the skull of a *raksha*. It was compact and very simple, made from clay.

The Guru also concealed *vajras* and *phurbas*, both powerful symbolic wrathful objects to cut through the dense negativity of these dark times. My first encounter with one of these very precious objects came by chance a few years ago in Nepal. I was in a monastery near the ancient Boudhnath Stupa. A Nepalese man was sitting quietly on the floor beside the cushioned seat of Chokyi Nyima Rinpoche, the seventh incarnation from the lineage of the Yogi-scholar Nagarjuna. An attendant carried into the room a large object completely wrapped up in an old stained cloth. I stared at the object, transfixed by it through its inelegant covering, and whispered to a friend – though I had no way of knowing this – 'It's Padmasambhava's *vajra*.'

Chokyi Nyima placed the covered object on the man's head and held it there for a few moments. The man changed position, his hands moving spontaneously in graceful *mudra* gestures. He rose and danced for a few minutes, moving his whole body in time with an inner rhythm. Then he sat down and became his normal self, unaware of the cosmic dance he had just been enacting. It was, as I had somehow known intuitively, a *vajra* belonging to Padmasambhava, a powerful *terma* treasure.

Later I learned how all these *vajras* and *phurbas* were made. It sounds incredible, but these are the bare facts, unadorned with mythologizing in any way. When Padmasambhava subdued the negative forces and local gods in Tibet, he transformed them into *dharma* protectors with particular areas of influence. Dorje Legpa was one of these local gods who became a wisdom protector entrusted with a special activity: to forge from pure sky metal the supernatural power objects which Padma would conceal as *terma*.

Sky metal or *namchak* is an iron-like metal formed atmospherically by the power of wind and fire. It is a solid substance, but it is *not* of this planet. 'It's like Excalibur', Tai Situpa explained. 'It's that type of thing, exactly the same kind of thing. It's not a human thing.'

Namchak cannot be kept for long by the wrong person: if someone tries to steal it, he can't keep it. There are stories of stolen sacred objects in Tibet that were returned because the person would start to vomit blood and become deathly ill, then have to bring it back. *Namchak* particularly, has a way of getting back to its rightful owner, the lama or devotee to whom it really *belongs*, who can rightfully possess it.

In one night Dorje Legpa forged one hundred *namchak phurbas*, and these were concealed as *terma*. Zilnon Lingpa told me about how one of these was returned to him. 'In my position I had many *terma phurbas* and *vajras*,' he said, 'but when I left Tibet many of these things were left behind. One of them was a *phurba* about a foot and a half long, made of *namchak*, with three heads. It was a *terma* taken from rock by Nuden Dorje about 190 years ago. During my last visit in 1985, it was returned to me. It is an interesting story.

'A monk from my monastery, called Lama Ugyen, showed me a *phurba* one day and asked, "Do you recognize this?"

'"Yes," I replied. "It's the Terchen's *phurba*. How did you manage to save it?" I asked him.

'"I kept it by not showing respect for it," he replied. "I used it as a stake to tie my horse to, so the Chinese would not suspect its preciousness. But it was only to keep it safely, so I do not think it is bad. Here," he said, handing it to me, "now you take it."'

Like Excalibur, *namchak* is sometimes brought by nonterrestial beings and handed to its rightful owner, one who has developed the power to keep it. While I was in Rumtek, Sangye

Nyenpa Rinpoche told me about a *phurba* he inherited from his previous incarnation, brought by a strange being from another realm, a non-human.

'One morning while he [the previous incarnation] was meditating at his retreat centre at Benchen Monastery, suddenly a "person" appeared. He was quite old with white hair and very ugly clothes. He did not speak any words at all. He just placed the *phurba* on the table, and in a moment he was gone. No one else in the monastery saw him.

'We call that kind of person *nimayin* – someone who looks like a person but actually is not. No person could keep the *phurba*,' he explained, 'so it had to be offered to someone who was highly developed.' At my request he reached into the cupboard of his shrine and brought it out, wrapped in an old cloth. When he touched it to my head there was a buzzing sensation, like electricity, and warmth.

'The *phurba* is the combination of all the buddhas' activities to destroy obstacles in a wrathful form,' His Holiness Sakya Trizin explained. His particular pure family lineage of the wrathful deity Vajrakilaya – who is actually the shape of a *phurba* – claims to have about twenty-one *namchak phurbas* that have been passed down from Padmasambhava. 'These are used only for the innermost circle of disciples,' he explained.

'Every one of the Vajrakilaya masters,' His Holiness said, 'has performed great miracles [with the phurba]: such as stabbing the *phurba* on rocks and water appears. When my grandfather was asked to perform the Vajrakilaya ritual at the palace of the Dalai Lama, actual nectar came from the *torma* of Vajrakilaya.'

'There is some *namchak* so powerful,' Thrangu Rinpoche told me, 'that if you put it on the head, one becomes cured.' I decided to return to Chokyi Nyima and asked him to explain the incident I had witnessed with the Nepalese man a few years before.

'The *vajra* heals physical and mental problems,' he said. 'At first I was almost afraid to use it [as it has so much power]. Sometimes people were fainting, sometimes falling unconscious for a few seconds. Some people think this is some kind of electric shock, like a charge. Some feel heat over their heads; some feel it going through their body to the feet. If something happens, then it is curing. If there's no experience, then nothing is happening.

'It works best through a combination of faith and power meeting together. If both meet together then it's very powerful. If there's not much faith but the object is very powerful, then the blessing is still strong. If there is no belief but still openness, it helps.

'But if there's wrong belief, then it is difficult. Wrong belief means this person thinks the object is really nothing. Then not much will happen when that person is touched with it. I can try, but it's very strange.

'There's another interesting story about this vajra,' he continued.

'In the afternoon I don't see people, so my monks tell a little lie – they lock the door from the outside and say that I am not in. One day a few people came, according to my attendant, two men who looked like very important ministers, and one woman who looked very strange.

'My monk said I was not in, but the woman insisted, "yes, he's there, I saw him."

' "How did you see him?" my attendant asked.

' "I know," she replied. Apparently she was psychic.

'So I was curious to see her, but at the same time I did not want them to know that I was the lama because we had already lied. So I just walked out looking not very special, the same as any of my monks.

'Immediately she grabbed my hand in a powerful grip. "You are the incarnation lama," she said, and would not let me go. She was very strong. "We need help from you. Till now I was helping these people but this time my power is not enough. You have the power," she pleaded. "Give me a blessing."

'So I put the *vajra* on her head. Her reaction was much greater than the Nepalese man whom you saw – strange words, dancing, gestures. Afterwards she prostrated to me very beautifully, precisely, three times.

' "Do you know who I am?" she asked.

' "I really don't know," I replied.

' "In the time of the Buddha I was a local deity, but ever since the Buddha gave teaching to me I have only wanted to help others. On one side of Swyamdbud there is a temple where many people go. That is where I stay."

'Then I understood that inside that lady there was another mind that came from Swyamdbud, and which even now stays in Swyamdbud and helps people, like a spirit. She was very powerful. Later I found out that she is quite famous.'

★ ★ ★

My longing to meet the Guru through his sacred legacy is intense. It is a feeling of having lost something and needing to go somewhere to be joined with it. When I hear about the *terma* collection of Chokgyur Lingpa it strikes a resonant chord, and I am compelled to make the pilgrimage to see it. I'm warned that it is guarded by his son Orgyan Tobgyal Rinpoche.

In the hushed early morning soon after the Tibetan New Year in March, I set out. The footpath to Bir from Sherabling goes through pine forest so evocatively still it seems sunk into primordial time; it crosses a river that tumbles from snow mountains into fields of green winter wheat where wild tulips splash white and crimson-coloured love-marks. Then, after traversing an expanse of open ground, the curved high roof of the monastery rises into view, the first exotic manmade landmark on the path.

My own path leads to the door of a large white house near the monastery. I have come with no credentials, and I am nobody. But the Vajra Guru mantra is my heartsong. Will the protector let me in to claim the legacy? Do I have the key to the door?

Orgyan Tobgyal opens the door, and keeps on opening it wider and wider. He places the collection on a table under a silk canopy. For the first time I see *namchak, vajras* and *phurbas* – immense, smooth, very simple, ancient, and truly not of this world: a miniature *kutshab* (regent) of the Guru and his two consorts, Mandarava and Yeshes Tsogyal, simple, like primitive art; a large dark metal bell belonging to King Trisong Detsen from the ancient time; and a startlingly perfect image in metal of the Guru staring directly into reality, transcending metal and paint, alive. Everything in me stops. As they are touched to my head, the presence of the Guru melts my heart.

This afternoon in the forest, time stretches out like an elastic band. 'Yesterday and a thousand years ago are the same to me, actually,' Tai Situpa had said. I glimpse his meaning. It is the deep eternal present, the limitless expanse.

The sound of birds echoing into space vibrates in my throat, the mandala of sound. Pine trees blur into wavy lines of wood colours; the wind has a new-born gossamer breath.

It feels as though I am coming home again.

V

◯

Spontaneous Expression

When the Karmapa was on his first tour of Europe, I heard he would be performing an important consecration ceremony at his land in the Dordogne. Immediately I determined to be there. Two of my close friends made a similar decision, so we hired an old ambulance which had been converted into a camper and put all our money into food, equipment and return tickets so that we would be entirely self-sufficient for the two-week period. And off we chugged – it was an old-fashioned Bedford van, heavy as a tank, with clumsy gears and a deafening diesel engine. I was the only driver in the group, and by the time we had cleared London's traffic, I realized how intensely I disliked driving it.

A few hundred miles south of Paris on the second exhausting day, without any warning, the ambulance came to a sudden halt and would go no further. A long black oily line on the road coming from under the vehicle showed the cause, and a further inspection revealed that the sump plug had come out, a most unusual occurrence. The oil had leaked out, the engine had seized – and that was the end of our carefully planned self-contained trip. Although it was strange to be suddenly 'homeless', I secretly welcomed the abrupt separation from this hot, cumbersome, noisy shell.

We seemed to be nowhere in particular; certainly there was no village in sight, just a farmhouse on one side of the road. But I saw a sign about twenty metres away and ran up to it to get our bearings. I gazed in disbelief at the words printed clearly before me. The sign spoke very plainly. It said, 'LA GRACE DE DIEU'. It was a very particular moment, thrilling actually. It seemed that the universe was speaking and, mysterious as it was, everything was happening as it should.

We abandoned the vehicle and hitch-hiked, which took two more days. By the time we reached the Dordogne, we all felt we had been through a special kind of preparation in which an outer skin was shed. Softened by divine grace, we entered the mandala of the Karmapa.

For me the Grace of God turned out to be a sign of guidance and protection on the path. I have been awestruck several times since by the striking language of synchronistic events with powerful, often unconscious emotions. And these events seem to arise solely in a spiritual context – 'in the presence of the Lord'.

This story is a personal example of a meaningful arrangement of events that seems to erupt spontaneously, bursting through the usual chain of causes and conditions. For this reason, serious research into this area is tricky: no pre-planned experiment can succeed, because causality is not a factor. The closest to scientific research I am aware of is Jung's essay, *Synchronicity: an Acausal Connecting Principle*. Jung was fascinated by these meaningful cross-connections, or synchronicity, because his own life provided him with startling examples. He developed some theories about it, and these illuminate certain sacred phenomena that occurred so frequently in Tibet they were almost common – self-arising or *rangjung* acts of spontaneous creation.

It is always dangerous to compare different systems. The Buddhist understanding of mind and matter is a unique and highly developed one, and does not interface with Jung's notion of a material universe. Having said that, I feel that his explanation of synchronicity can be a window for the Western-trained intellect into understanding this important phenomenon.

According to Jung, there are two quite different ways that events are related to one another. The first and ordinary way is as a causal chain, A–B–C–D, one event producing another. The other is more like a web than a line, with meaningful cross-connections arising spontaneously. 'Synchronicity,' Jung says, 'is a concept that formulates a point of view diametrically opposed to that of causality.'[1]

The synchronistic view produces a meaningful picture of what looks like coincidence.

> How does it happen that A–B–C–D, etc. appear all in the same moment and in the same place? It happens in the first place because the

physical events A and B are of the same quality as the psychic events C and D, and further because all are the exponents of one and the same momentary situation.[2]

In other words, a powerful psychic image, symbol, or thought takes a material expression spontaneously owing to the mutual attraction of related objects.

Synchronicity thus involves two factors, says Jung.

> a) An unconscious image comes into consciousness either directly (i.e. literally), or indirectly (symbolized or suggested) in the form of a dream, idea, or premonition. b) An objective situation coincides with this content.[3]

'Unlike causality,' he continues, 'synchronicity is a phenomenon that seems to be primarily connected with psychic conditions, that is to say, with processes in the unconscious.'[4]

What exactly are these processes in the unconscious? Jung described the collective unconscious as a receptacle of innate, primordial knowledge which nothing has caused. Archetypes constitute the structure of the collective unconscious. They are 'formal factors responsible for the organization of unconscious psychic processes ... At the same time they have a specific "charge."'[5] The forms of inherent psychic orderedness — or archetypes — are also 'introspectively recognizable'. Since we all have certain electric or magnetic powers to attract or repel within us, the 'specific charge' of the archetype can be released into consciousness as an interaction forms. 'Certain phenomena of simultaneity or synchronicity seem to be bound up with the archetypes,' concludes Jung;[6] and he expands the definition of synchronicity accordingly. It is an 'acausal orderedness'.

What actually makes an event synchronistic is the meeting that comes together at one point in time. Simultaneously occurring events demonstrate a kind of spontaneous ordering that is deeply creative. It is important to understand the implications underlying synchronistic phenomena, because what they really reveal is that there is no authentic division of time into three parts — past, present and future. As Jung understood very well, space and time in themselves consist of nothing; they are simply concepts 'born of the discriminating activity of the conscious mind'. Useful, in fact indispensable, in describing certain events such as the behaviour of bodies in motion, in relation to the psyche 'space and time are, so to speak, elastic ... and can apparently be reduced almost to vanishing point, as though they were dependent on psychic conditions and did not exist in themselves.'[7]

When we apply all this Jungian research to Buddhist sacred phenomena, it is possible to glimpse mystic reality with the rational mind. A simple but quite revolutionary statement emerges: that there are formal patterns in the innate mind which, through the power of meditation, devotion, prayer or 'presence' can externalize materially, or manifest in nature spontaneously; and these acts of creation come into being authentically, when the time is right. The natural creative act, says Jung, must be regarded as 'the continuous creation of a pattern that exists from all eternity, repeats itself sporadically, and is not derivable from any known antecedents.'[8]

The sacred mandala that was Tibet produced a spiritual culture in which the archetype was so conscious, so recognized, that nature manifested it spontaneously, and frequently. 'We call it *rangjung*,' said Zilnon Lingpa, 'because there's no description of cause and effect.' Nor has there been any scholarly research into it, no in-depth historical description in the scriptures, in Padmasambhava's writings or those of any of his disciples to theorize how it is produced, nothing to give it a causal definition. It is there and no one has made it.

Ten years ago when I first went on pilgrimage in Nepal, I was fascinated by a formation in the rock, strewn with white offering scarves, where Tibetan pilgrims were lighting incense and butter lamps in devotion. It was easy to see the rough shape of a seated figure with the right leg extended and slightly bent. No humanly made sculpture could imitate this because the form was pushing *out* of the rock with all its naturally rough texture; and some parts were clear, some not yet properly formed. Last year I returned there and this time the form was distinct, quite complete – the female deity of compassion, the great mother, Green Tara.

I discovered that Tara has been coming out of this rock more and more clearly for the past twenty years or so, the sign of Tara herself in this place. It is said that even the winds that touch the miraculously forming image transmit her blessing. And when there are no longer great masters to impart the teaching, the image will remain – to remind us of the inherent forms of our authentic being.

Rangjung is a process that depends on our readiness to receive its message. When the time is right to 'speak', the image will emerge more and more clearly. At the close of the *kalpa*, though, when Sakyamuni's teaching dies out on this planet, *rangjung* images and mantras will recede into the rock, vanishing without trace. The web of consciousness interlocking all existence is truly expressive.

'There's only *rangjung* if there's a *knower* of the *rangjung*,' Dzongsar Khyentse Rinpoche pointed out, cutting to the heart of the phenomenon. 'There won't be any under the sea, because there's no point in having *rangjung* under the sea. *Rangjung* is auspicious,' he summarized, 'if there are human beings who are going to benefit from that *rangjung*.'

Naturally, the particular form that is beneficial depends on the propensity of the perceiver, on the thought forms of a culture and the images that arise out of it. For example, a Tara suddenly appears in the rock in Tibet or Nepal, where everybody believes in Tara. 'It's the result of a group karma,' Khyentse Rinpoche explained. 'It's a group energy.' Our discussion showed the interlocking factors.

'So it's like the thought forms that are current in a particular civilization and the strong power of devotion?'

'It's group karma, just that. A manifestation of group energy.'

'So Tara will never appear in the rock in the West until everybody believes in Tara?'

'Or quite a number of people.'

'Could you also say that it comes to that place because a yogi is there doing practice and his visualization is so strong...'

The reply came before I could finish my question: 'But in order for such a kind of yogi to come there, you again need group energy.'

Group energy: the power of thought forms, the mind-stream of a culture which attracts certain phenomena. There are many inexplicable things for which we have no rational scientific explanation: the Easter Islands, Stonehenge, the Great Pyramid. But in our culture, they are part of our mythology, the mystery of their formation buried in a previous stratum of mind. Only uncovering our original nature can reveal it; what is needed is an archaeology of the mind.

In Tibet, where common people uttered mantra as naturally as breathing from the time they could form words, and recognized Chenresig and Tara as they would their father and mother, mantra and image appeared spontaneously on rock and caves. Since a *rangjung* sacred image or syllable is not a haphazard event, but a special blessing to liberate beings – a sign of buddhas' activity – it can arise only in relation to a particular group energy. In Buddhist terminology, this is called merit.

At Rumtek Monastery in Sikkim, I asked the great scholar Gyaltsap Rinpoche to describe the circumstances of *rangjung* and its meaning. 'These things are inconceivable, beyond our imagination,' he replied. 'It's difficult to explain logically how it happens, but it's a fact that we find *rangjung* in different places, in caves and on rocks, and it has a connection with particular bodhisattvas and yogis.' Then he offered a detailed description of how the immaterial could manifest in the fullness of time.

'It can happen when a master is performing a special prayer or making an offering to a particular deity. During that time the deity appears to the *vajra* master, and he is invited to sit there. Because of the power of the master, the deity dissolves or sinks into the place where he has been asked to sit. In this way, the impression of his form becomes "concealed", and after some years it comes out. This is an example of how these things happen,' he revealed.

Another way it has been known to manifest is during a group practice involving several powerful masters. Around the beginning of this century, four renowned *tertons* performed an elaborate week-long *mendrup*, a ceremony for consecrating *dutsi* or sacred medicine. When the 1st Jamgon Kongtrul, the 14th Karmapa, the 1st Khyentse and the third Chokling Rinpoches performed the *mendrup* of Padmasambhava, the medicine became so empowered that an image of the Guru in union with his consort was born spontaneously from the medicine. The 14th Karmapa took it and it is now kept as one of the sacred treasures of Rumtek.

'Different images which arise spontaneously or naturally,' Gyaltsap Rinpoche explained, 'are all produced by the power of meditation and the power of blessing of different buddhas and bodhisattvas.' But the circumstances that make this expression arise have to do with more than the power of the master alone: it is the merit of beings. 'If it's only concerned with the master,' he emphasized, 'then the buddhas always have the compassion and power to turn every rock into some blessing. But beings must have enough merit and fortune to benefit from it.'

The places in nature where *rangjung* happens are significant indications: at Dhongri Mountain in Tibet, sacred to the protector Mahakala, there is a large *rangjung* image of the six-armed Mahakala; in Ladakh near the boundary with Kashmir a huge Maitreya

Buddha has appeared out of the rock, standing like a sentinel to the Buddhist realm. The turquoise worn round the neck of King Songsten Gampo, the first Buddhist king of Tibet, manifested the form of Green Tara, naturally. At Palpung Monastery in Kham, seat of the Tai Situpas, Vajra Yogini's whole body manifested spontaneously on a red rock. 'It's small but absolutely perfect,' Tai Situpa told me, 'a clear Vajra Yogini standing. There are many things like that,' he reflected.

'What are the factors involved in that?' I asked.

'It's many, many things,' he said with authority. 'One important thing is the event that *has* happened in that particular place; or the event that *will* happen in that particular place. If something fantastic were going to happen in this valley – if this place were going to be the seat of real Buddhist practice, Vajrayana practice, for the next hundred years – there would be many things coming up in advance, spontaneously.'

'How do you account for that in terms of dependent arising?' I asked. An omen seems even more incredible than a past event. How can nature 'know' the future?

'Whatever is happening is so powerful that even nature manifests it,' he replied.

'Do you mean, for example,' I asked, 'that the *rangjung* lake that manifested when Yeshes Tsogyal was born is nature manifesting the occurrence?'

'Definitely.'

The rational Western-orientated part of me finds this difficult to assimilate, as though it was not developed to take in that kind of fact. 'That's something that in Western culture we almost can't understand, it's a little bit inconceivable.'

'Some part of the brain is more developed for a certain type of historical background, and another part is more developed for a different type of historical background. In Western culture your historical background might not have too many of these things, so your brain is not developed in that area. For Tibetans, it is in their culture, in their blood. It's in their system.'

'So these phenomena are more likely to form in a place like Tibet?'

'Definitely. But it doesn't mean it cannot manifest anywhere else. Right now in the West when the *dharma* is flourishing, many things can happen there also.' He paused for a moment and added, 'I'm surprised that there isn't any holy place developed yet in the West for Buddhism – not just an emotional aspect, but something real.'

Perhaps there is, I suggested. On the same day that the Karmapa was cremated at Rumtek monastery, some inexplicable phenomena occurred at the place in Wales where he had performed the Black Crown ceremony seven years earlier. From Karmapa's photograph, a chest where *dharma* texts were kept, the floor near the throne where he had sat, and on the Mahakala shrine, water suddenly appeared. Remembering a special longevity turquoise Tai Situpa had described to me, which during long-life prayers would produce water, I asked if this occurrence was also auspicious. 'It could be something,' he agreed.

Changing direction suddenly, he said emphatically, '*Rangjung* means spontaneously arising.' He paused a moment. 'It does not mean good or bad. Something terrible can also be *rangjung*.' I listened amazed as he developed the reverse aspect. 'I will say that when Europe was supposed to have the worst time of humanity, then Hitler was born. This is a kind of example, you know.'

'But that was not a *rangjung* phenomenon' I protested, incredulous.

'Yes,' he replied. 'It was also *rangjung*. No parents would want their son to be like Hitler. He was *rangjung*. Definitely. He just came about.'

There are many periods in history where nature manifested extreme negative energy in the form of natural cataclysms: portents of doom in the night skies, like comets, and in the earth's crust, like earthquakes. In a culture as spiritually integrated as Tibet, one could expect that the most dire period in its history – the Chinese Communist invasion – would be marked by *rangjung* phenomena. And it was.

One night in 1950, two months before the invasion, throughout the length and breadth of Tibet, people experienced an unprecedented natural phenomenon – an earthquake accompanied by thirty or forty explosions, and a strange red glow in the skies in the direction from which the noise came. The Dalai Lama, a firm believer in scientific investigation, tried to find a rational explanation for it. But there was none. 'My own feeling,' he recorded in his memoirs, 'is that what happened is presently beyond science, something truly mysterious. In this case I find it much easier to accept that what I witnessed was metaphysical.'[9] From that time onwards, the situation in Tibet rapidly worsened.

There were other signs, of a more particular nature. On his departure from Ganden Monastery before his first journey to Communist China, the Dalai Lama noticed 'something very strange.' A statue of one of the protector deities of Tibet, usually with a peaceful expression and looking downwards, had changed position. 'Now,' he observed, 'it was facing east with a very ferocious expression.'[10] Even more sinister, at the time of his escape into exile, the walls of a chapel at Ganden ran with blood.

Powerful energy thus expresses itself naturally, and as it does, it expands our vision of reality, of the 'way it is', in itself, without concept. The view is of an intricate web of interdependent systems, a vast interlocking sensitive network in which consciousness, energy and matter penetrate each other. Places, especially sacred places, acquire an inherent memory or storage of energy. And this may be released, expressing itself synchronistically with a powerful past or future event. So the walls of Ganden, where prayers to benefit every particle of sentient life throughout the infinite cosmos had permeated the rock, wept tears of blood.

Supreme of all places in storing consciousness and energy is the body itself. So the body of a great yogi, a spiritual master who has spent all his life in meditation, one who has realized boundaryless consciousness or non-ego, is a very special, auspicious form. When consciousness leaves at the time of death, the body becomes an especially holy place and produces various kinds of *rangjung* formations.

The death of a spiritual master is a powerful event. There is no fear or agony in the death process because there is no ego to die. What happens is natural: the child merges with the mother, the created dissolves into the uncreated – the great expanse. The stages leading up to death, the moment of death itself, and the stages after it, are called the *tuk dam*, or final meditation. The *tuk dam*, in which the mind remains in the 'clear light' and enlightenment is attained, generally lasts three days, but it can last weeks or longer. For the entire duration of the *tuk dam*, the meditator, though sitting upright and appearing vibrant, is clinically dead. The process is often witnessed by certain fortunate disciples and it always has a greatly transfiguring effect.

Because it is such an unmistakable indicator of spiritual realization, and the ground for the formation of *rangjung*, appreciating the significance of this event can expand one's understanding immediately. For this reason, I am now sharing some information that is usually restricted, concerning the great yogi and spiritual master, Kalu Rinpoche, who, on 10 May 1989, 'passed from this world into the pure realms'.

In an open letter circulated to all his disciples, Bokar Rinpoche, who witnessed the passing into final meditation, describes the *tuk dam*. At the point his description begins, Kalu Rinpoche had suffered a heart attack, his lungs were working at only 40 percent capacity, and he was put on oxygen and given glucose intravenously. He made several attempts to sit upright but was prevented from doing so by the doctors. Finally, realizing that it was his final meditation, his close disciples helped him; he made a gesture with his hand that he wished to sit absolutely straight. These are the words of Bokar Rinpoche.

> Rinpoche placed his hands in meditation posture, his open eyes gazed outwards in meditation gaze, and his lips moved softly. A profound feeling of peace and happiness settled on us all and spread through our minds. All of us present felt that the indescribable happiness filling us was the faintest reflection of what was pervading Rinpoche's mind. Lama Gyaltsen also felt a passing experience of the profound sorrow characteristic of compassionate awareness of the suffering pervading cyclic existence. This also was felt to be a gift of Rinpoche's awareness. Slowly Rinpoche's gaze and his eyelids lowered and the breath stopped...
>
> I have been witness to a number of people passing from this world. Occasionally there is a short rasping breath, occasionally a long inhalation or exhalation. With Rinpoche there was none of these: a most extraordinary passing into profound meditation.

The disciples took care that the environment was quiet and Rinpoche left undisturbed for the duration of the *tuk dam*. A few hours later, Jamgon Kongtrul Rinpoche arrived, followed later in the evening by Shamar Rinpoche. 'Both remarked how vital Rinpoche's form was, as though any moment he might begin to speak.' On the morning of the third day, all the signs indicating that the *tuk dam* was complete had appeared. As they washed the body and changed the clothes, they noted that there was no trace of body waste or impurity, and that the body remained soft and flexible without any stiffness.

A decision was taken not to cremate the body (known as *ku dung*), but to prepare it as a *mar dung* so that it would always remain, a tradition practised in Tibet. 'In this way,' Bokar Rinpoche explained, 'the physical aspect of the lama's form remains as a relic, a basis for religious inspiration. Thus the lama's activity continues as beings are liberated through seeing, hearing, considering, touching or praising the relic of his *mar dung*.' Every kind of connection with it becomes beneficial – even a negative one. This is due to the tremendous power of the lama's *bodhicitta*, the enlightened wish to liberate beings with every cell, every pore of his being.

When the body is cremated, this enlightened wish becomes formations that arise naturally in the bone. Some of the most famous of these are the special forms of Chenresig that appeared in the rib bones of the great Tibetan *mahasiddha*, Tsangpa Gyare. 'There are twenty-one *rangjung* formations that came from the ribs,' Sed Rinpoche disclosed. 'One of the most precious ones is in Bhutan, in Punakha Dzong. I think it's Karsapani – it's not the thousand-armed Chenresig. I went to see this. It was in a small *gow*. It changes colour, which indicates that something is going to happen. At that time it was a little bit bluish.'

'How would you explain a *rangjung* formation like that?' I asked Rinpoche.

'I can only say from my own observation. Tsangpa Gyare wrote a prayer which says, in part, "When I am enlightened, may my body benefit all sentient beings, even a single hair or pore of my skin, or ash – may each of them benefit sentient beings." So he had that kind of strong *bodhicitta* aspiration; and when he died, he succeeded. His bones manifested spontaneously into Chenresig. So he fulfilled his aspiration to benefit sentient beings through his body.' He paused.

I knew he possessed one of these *rangjung* formations of Tsangpa Gyare. 'Does the one you have change colour?' I asked.

'No.' Then he confessed, 'I also have a bone of Phagmo Drukpa, the founder of the Drukpa Kagyud. It's a shin bone and you can see it's a *rangjung* Tara.' At my request, he brought out both relics. Opening the cloth, he cautioned, 'I never show this. If you go to Bhutan you have to get very special permission.' I beheld a long bone, very clean and shiny. At first when I looked at it my vision was not subtle enough to notice what was there. Turning it slightly, I saw inside the bone, fine and slender as a needle, a perfect miniature of the thousand-armed Chenresig, every intricate detail etched clearly in the bone. The bone of Phagmo Drukpa was completely white and showed the clear form of Tara as though it had been carved into ivory.

There are many famous *rangjung* formations. Another one is the seed syllable of Manjushri formed in the rib bone of the 8th Karmapa. More recently, when the 16th Karmapa was cremated in 1981, some of the ashes were distributed to devotees. Drupon Dechen Rinpoche noticed some time after receiving his blessing that an image was forming in a bone from the shin. It became a very clear image of Sakyamuni Buddha.

'There's *rangjung* on bones, in the forehead, like on skulls,' Tai Situpa revealed. 'I have seen many things: skulls that have the eight auspicious signs, skulls that have *AH*. I have the skull of a person whose name isn't known, with the Tibetan letter *AH*, absolutely perfect; handwriting couldn't be better. It's a spontaneous *AH* and it's on a bone from the skull.'

'Does this have some particular significance in terms of the realization of that person?' I asked.

'Of course it describes something. It's the *nirmanakaya* of that person which was left for future generations. *AH* represents emptiness, so maybe that person was a practitioner of *prajna paramita*, or any *yidam* (deity) that has the syllable *AH*. The seed syllable is the alphabetical representation of the deity. If someone attains realization of his *yidam*, then that particular syllable just appears naturally. That is one thing it can show. Another thing it can show is that the person has been concentrating on a certain image his whole life. The mind is so powerful that whatever point he was concentrating on, the shape forms physically. Reaching the realization of the *yidam*, manifesting it physically, is much higher than the second one. But it can be anything,' he emphasized.

The only documented evidence on the entire subject that I have been able to uncover is a quotation from the Indian master Atisa, which explains with scholarly exactitude what the different *rangjung* images signify. I read it aloud: 'Deity images occur to those who have mastered the Generation Stage contemplations. For those of pure conduct, there are rains of flowers. When *bodhicitta* is highly developed, *ringsel* drip out. When the letter *AH* occurs, it demonstrates mastery of the inner and outer sensory potentialities (*ayatana*). For non-returners, a spiralling conch occurs. In the case of bodhisattvas who have not abandoned *samsara*, hearts and tongues occur.'[11]

Tai Situpa's response was to break the boundaries of scientific classification, to open it up to the spontaneous, the unprecedented – the causeless. 'You can use that sort of thing,' he replied, 'but you can't be too specific about it. It's just a guideline, it's not a law. You should not be too rigid about it. Anything can be anything,' he said a second time.

One thing it certainly shows though: that the practitioner has meditated so effectively and completely on this sacred syllable that it has reproduced itself spontaneously on his skull. Specifically, it means the practitioner has uncovered the seed syllable within. According to the Tantric teaching, seed syllables are sacred letters residing within the subtle nerve centres of the body, corresponding to the gross perceptions and projections which create *samsara*. By meditating on the seed syllables – the innately pure source of appearance – gross perceptions are transformed into refined, pure being; and the projections that have chained us to *samsara* dissolve. The seed syllable is thus the source of liberation: projections are wound back into it, returned to origin. The imprint on the skull is the sure sign that the seed syllable has been uncovered, recognized, and liberated.

In his memoirs, the Dalai Lama reveals that he was shown a relic of his guru, Tathag Rinpoche: a piece of the skull that had survived the flames. On it was imprinted the Tibetan syllable that corresponded to his protector divinity – the pure form born from the seed syllable. 'This mysterious phenomenon,' he notes, 'is quite common amongst high lamas. The bones melt in such a way as to reveal characters, or sometimes images. In other cases, such as that of my predecessor, those imprints can actually be observed on the body itself.'[12] It is simply the shape of profound truth, uncreated by anyone.

As well as *rangjung* images and letters in the bones, there is another significant kind of relic that is often discovered in the ashes of a realized master: *ringsel*. One type is a very tiny, round calcid substance about the size of a mustard seed, the unmistakable sign of a bodhisattva – one who benefits beings on a totally selfless, compassionate level. Another type is bigger, very polished and bright, found in the five primary colours representing the five buddha activities. This is produced only from the bones of someone who is enlightened, like a buddha. This kind is said to be unbreakable even if pounded in an iron mortar. 'If we try to break it with a hammer,' said Zilnon Lingpa, 'even with a blacksmith's anvil, it's not possible. Sacred *ringsel* is indestructible.'

Ringsel is the material essence of realization, a natural 'gift'. Tai Situpa described its cause: 'It is due to the great realization of that person, so its presence will be available for many people; and it comes out in a most pure, precious and convenient form.'

Sed Rinpoche told me a story about the spontaneous formation of *ringsel* from the saliva of the Karmapa. 'Once when the Karmapa was in a garden he spat on to a leaf. A devotee who was watching folded the leaf and put it into his *gow*. Five or so years later he opened the *gow* and *ringsel* was coming out of it, little white bones.

He was very surprised since he hadn't put *ringsel* into it. So he opened the dry leaf and saw that it was full of ringsel.'

Because *ringsel* is meant to benefit as many beings as possible, all good genuine *ringsel* will multiply miraculously if it is kept properly and treated with respect. Otherwise, it may disappear. I asked Lodro Thaye, a monk and possessor of some precious *ringsel* – seven of them given by the master Tulku Urgyen – whether any of his *ringsel* had multiplied. 'When I heard that it would multiply,' he replied, 'I used to look quite frequently to see. Then I thought mine weren't going to reproduce, so I didn't look for a long time – quite a few years. Then last time I counted very carefully and saw that there were more. There were well over forty. Though I can't remember how many I'd been given, it certainly wasn't that amount.

'One thing Tulku Urgyen said,' he continued, 'is that the *ringsel* produced by his father, which he wore around his neck, multiplied all the time. His father had been a married lama who practised very strongly and produced about seventy or eighty *ringsel* when he died.'

The amount of *ringsel* produced – whether less, or more, or any at all – depends largely on the devotion of the disciples and how pure their commitment is. It is an accurate measure of something intangible: sincerity. When the universe 'speaks,' its voice is always authentic.

When the Buddha passed into Nirvana, his disciples found enough *ringsel* from his ashes to fill eight pots. These were distributed to the various great kings of India who built massive dome-like shapes, or *stupas*, to contain and honour the precious substances. The relics of the Buddha multiplied and spread to every Buddhist country. In Burma a new *stupa* has been built specifically as a museum of *ringsel*, showing the different colours and sizes – up to a quarter of an inch in diameter.

At Palpung Monastery in Tibet, there is the *ringsel* of Sakyamuni Buddha – very tiny and round. But more extraordinary, there is also the relic of Dipankara, the Buddha previous to Sakyamuni – a substance around two million years old. 'It's huge,' Tai Situpa said, 'about the size of an egg – white and very oddly shaped, like a real heart shape with holes in it. But it's *ringsel*, something that was born from his body after he died. It shines and is very lively, alive.

'Another important thing in Palpung,' he continued, 'is Gampopa's finger – just the top of the finger bone. Once in a while a small, white, very shiny relic comes out of it. This is *ringsel*, produced by the finger.'

As with *rangjung* images, it is not only the bones of realization that 'speak', but also certain natural formations and sacred structures where the resonance of veneration has permeated the rock. Mount Kailash in western Tibet is called Kang Rinpoche, Precious Mountain, because from its lime, calcium and salt, *ringsel* forms. Swyanbud Stupa in Nepal which contains the relics of Dipankara Buddha, is famous for producing *ringsel*. 'Early one morning about fifteen or so years ago,' Lodro Thaye told me, 'when the lamas were circumambulating the *stupa*, the *ringsel* started coming out of it. They just started to appear on the pavement encircling it – little white pearls, very, very small. Quite a few people were there picking them up.'

Is there such a thing as objective intrinsic power? Or does the power of the mind, the strength of devotion, produce miraculous substance? Usually it is both – a generative interaction between mind and object of devotion. But there is an oft-told Tibetan tale, a true story, which shows clearly the supremacy of mind in transforming matter.

There was a simple village woman in Tibet whose son was about to journey to India on business. With great sincerity, she urged him to bring back a precious relic from the land of the Buddha. Months later he returned – alas, empty-handed. In the rush of commerce, he had forgotten all about it. Some time later he made preparations for a second trip; again she implored him to bring back a holy relic – and on no account to forget! She was getting old and there was not much time before death would come.

On his return journey, the son was approaching his home when he suddenly remembered his old mother's urgent request. Once again he had forgotten! It was too late to bring back anything from India, but he knew he dare not walk in empty-handed. Seeing a dog's tooth on the road, he picked it up, wrapped it carefully in the finest silk, and presented it ceremoniously to his mother as a relic of the Buddha. She was overjoyed to have such a powerful object of devotion. With great veneration, she placed it prominently on her shrine, making heart-felt prostrations and prayers to it every day. Her devotion increased immeasurably. One day she noticed that the tooth had produced little white round substances – *ringsel*. At her death she attained rainbow body.

If extreme positive energy can produce *ringsel* from a dog's tooth, how does extreme negative energy express itself? 'There are many kinds of *ringsel*,' Jamgon Kongtrul Rinpoche said. 'There are different shapes, different qualities. A lot of people bring *ringsel* from Tibet, but we are able to know the different kinds, not just from the material shape and colour, but also from its feeling. It is nothing to do with something you can learn from anybody, it has to come from your own experience: realization.'

He paused a few moments. 'You know, after death,' he continued, 'some teachers stay in meditation for three or four days, sometimes weeks, or longer – and this is considered very, very special. If we look into it, there are many different signs – just sitting up at death isn't necessarily a sign of realization.

'I want to tell you a story.' He paused a moment and added, 'It's a true story. There was a hunter who had hunted since childhood. When he died, though, he sat up in meditation – I don't know if it was exactly the meditation posture, but at least he was sitting up.

'Then people felt it was very strange because he'd been hunting, and killing is the most negative thing you can do. So they invited a lama, explained who he was, and so on. The lama was a very good meditator, and told them to shout at the dead body: "Now your deer has run away!"

'So they did. As soon as someone shouted it, the man fell down! Why? Because he had been fixating through fear. He had good concentration from shooting all his life, but no compassion. Anybody can have concentration; and in fact, concentration *is* required for meditation, but then meditation also has to have the *quality* of concentration.

'That's why it's necessary when judging these things to check everything, and it's really essential to have some experience yourself.

'You see,' he said meaningfully, answering my question directly, 'even pigs can have relics. You can find it in their flesh – a clear sign that this pig has been born nine life-times as a pig. Pigs represent ignorance. If you eat that relic, you can be reborn as a pig.'

'What happens if you eat the relics of a holy person?' I asked.

'It goes straight here,' he said, pointing to the top of his head. 'To the crown chakra. It opens it up. Normally we don't eat it till the time of death.'

★ ★ ★

When twilight touches Baudhanath and the chill rays of the dying sun linger on the massive dome, we circumambulate the Great

Stupa – I mean the stream of humanity linked with the heartbeat of that sacred place at that particular moment, and me; because sometimes I am also there. My mantra becomes part of the electric buzz that passes into the huge round body of the dome; my footsteps add the weight of one more human to the time-worn stones, the path circling the mammoth womb that represents the mind of the buddhas. I become submerged in the deeper current here, the subterranean flow that carries us surely to join the great heart of all the buddhas.

The *stupa* has been here from beginningless time – a previous *kalpa* – which is so long ago historically, it is really irrelevant to calculate it. For me it is more like an enlightened artefact than an historical construction. But according to the Legend – which was revealed as a *terma* text – the original structure was built by a simple poultry woman who had accumulated some wealth and wished to do just one good deed before she died. She acquired so much merit from this monumental act that, though she did not live to complete the project, at her death she attained rainbow body. And her three sons, who brought her wish to completion, incarnated countless thousands of years later as the King, the Abbot, and the Lotus-Born Guru who planted the Vajrayana in Tibet.

Wherever one goes in Baudha, the stupa rises up, a lighthouse in the sea of humanity struggling to get free. The eyes seem to follow one everywhere, enormous wide-awake petals of compassion, from whom nothing is hidden, everything forgiven. At twilight they exert a magnetic pull, and the tired heart of humankind floods in to shelter in their wisdom.

Humanity on the move, so many feet. Bandaged, maimed, twisted feet; tiny wizened bare feet; stumps. And no feet, just a torso struggling, heaving in the dust. The invisible ones, no name no home, no future, are moving. The claims of the mute, the wretched, the living dead, strangled during the day, touch the world of the living at twilight.

I am invisible this time, well nurtured, clothed, sheltered. My step is sure, my brain functions, mind and breath are balanced, my voice is heard. Precious – but it doesn't really become precious until I realize that it is. Leprous faces shrinking with plague extend gnarled stumps. Clink. Into the hungry bowl. I know what it is like to have no home, to feel fear, to be alone, to call out and get no reply, to weep and to die. I was invisible once too, not long ago, not far away, though my memory is somehow a little dim.

I merge with the maroon robes of the monks, an island of sanity in the black *bardo* sea. We turn the colossal prayer wheel, like captains of consciousness steering the ship to the other shore. With each revolution a gong reverberates through the womb. Lighting butter lamps in the darkness till the little prayer room is ablaze, we communicate in mantra with the *stupa*.

If the heart of the Buddha hadn't opened in me, if I hadn't melted into it just a little bit, the story would be entirely different.

'The self is always hungry, looking for power. It's a kind of food, a feeling of identity, security.' Flickering lights from the butter lamps on the shrine reflect on to Tarthang Tulku's face. A deep world-weariness seems to permeate his powerful presence. 'There's always hope that something will come,' he continues. 'Hope is symbolically positive thought, but if you look behind it, it means you are maintaining attachment – grasping, wishing. So what's going on with your mind? You're in a state of continual hunger, a state of continual punishment; thirsting, suffering – an eternal slave to your *self*. But you're determined. You don't give up, It'is absolutely fundamental. If you give up, you lose your identity; and if the self isn't there, what's it all for?'

We are in the uppermost chamber of a six-storey monastery in Baudha, a little removed from the *stupa*, but still the eyes of the Buddha look into the room. 'Fantasies, imagination, ideas, feelings, thoughts . . .' He pauses, his voice so low, so reflective, I can barely hear the words. 'Reality is different,' he says, almost to himself.

Night is closing in, the room darkens. The chanting of the monks below stops abruptly. There is a sudden intimacy of two people sharing the same place. 'Bittersweet,' I reply, acknowledging the taste of this moment. 'In my experience, when you really taste reality, it's bittersweet – some beauty, and some sadness.'

He looks up at me with interest. 'Did you really have that? Don't you think it's a human characteristic?' I nod. 'That process made you richer, brought you experience. This leads to knowledge. Eventually you become wise. But to have great wisdom born from that, it's very seldom – East or West, there's very few people.'

'Do you think there's an explanation for supernatural phenomena?' I ask, steering the conversation to my main area of interest. Tarthang Tulku is probably the foremost Tibetan lama to transpose Buddhist metaphysics into scientific idiom, so I am interested in his answer.

'Yes, I think so, but the only way to introduce the rational mind to it is through a mathematical language not through words. Science is technically too advanced to make an interpretive explanation. There are only a few who can work on that level, very few Westerners.

'Sometimes paranormal psychology can explain it a little,' he continues. 'In terms of specific units of power, every part has its own properties, its own life energy. For example, our eye has a different property from our heart. Sometimes we call it love, sometimes compassion, sometimes hate. They are all powerful emotional events. Somewhere it takes on a physical aspect – art is a very special one. Certain images and objects have their own units of energy, their own intrinsic value.'

Except for the light from the butter lamps and a faint glow from the window in the direction of the *stupa*, the room is completely dark. I narrate the story of my journey to Ladakh many years before, when I had the auspicious experience of *rangjung* in reverse. 'How would you explain dematerialization?'

'There are many explanations, but one thing is sure: there is no intentionality, no doing this way or that way. The buddhas don't have intention. A miracle happens ... or doesn't happen. Sometimes the *dharmapalas* [protectors] manifest in that way, so that is one possibility. Another possibility is that the blessing, or the power of the energy, and you have a connection. There are a lot of famous things like that which have happened in many monasteries – statues have talked, or they have disappeared. So maybe through your energy, your thought forms, you're plugging into it.'

'When something dematerializes, does it mean the energy is used up, the material form is used up, somehow?'

'I don't know. There's an arrangement, these are the facts. Is there cause and effect? Or no cause and effect?'

Finally we have reached the point, formulated the question, arrived at what I really wanted to understand. 'Is it spontaneous phenomena?'

He becomes vague. 'Something like that, yes. Phenomena.'

'Or is it possible to understand it with cause and effect? That it was connected with this very dangerous journey and we could have died; and this was a way of saving us, of absorbing the negative energy?'

'Yes, true.' He stops the flow of speculation: fantasies, imaginings, thoughts, feelings. 'One thing is,' he says pointedly, 'that you do not need to report it back to anyone. Don't you think it's interesting to you? Convincing to your own mind? That's all you need to know. If you try to figure it out, you may not find any answers.'

I understand so deeply what he is saying, it is almost as if my inner dialogue is being projected outwardly. The story has remained within me for twelve years, uninterruptedly dormant, a seed of knowledge that was taking its own time to grow. It has come out through a need to communicate authentic reality – but I feel the danger intuitively. 'I know,' I reply, 'but it's opened up something also.'

'I understand.' His voice is gentle, soft as the darkness that has gathered around us. 'But it may not happen again.'

VI

Buddha Activity

1. MAPPING THE MIND

All the special sacred objects that come into being represent buddha activity in its various forms. And all the ways that buddha energy manifests in objects, whether through sacred empowerment, secret revelation or spontaneous expression, arise in the context of a very special and particular container: the Vajrayana. So before examining the contents – buddha activity – it is useful to look at the container: the path of the *vajra*.

The *vajra* is the symbol of indestructibility, that which nothing can destroy. The reason it cannot be destroyed is that it was not *created* by anyone. It is fundamentally, inherently, authentically *there*. But it has been covered up, layered over, 'disowned'. 'We are buddha by nature,' Tai Situpa explained, 'and our surroundings are the realm of the buddha by nature. This is a pure realm; the ultimate essence of this is a pure land. So when we practise we try to become what we actually are.' This means that when all the conditions have been gathered, through practising the path, buddha nature emerges. That is the indestructibility that the *vajra* symbolizes.

It is so important to understand this because what it really means is that the *dharma* of the Buddha, the Awakened One, has more to do with psychology than with religion – psychology so profound, so far-reaching, it has never been surpassed; and this psychology has acquired over thousands of years the status of a religion. It is a purely modern distinction, though. In Tibet there were neither of these compartments because Tibetans were not exposed to other cultures. 'It just developed,' said Tai Situpa, 'and it was quite natural for everybody. As natural as it is to put food into your mouth when you eat, so when we pray we put our hands together. There is nothing foreign about it. Nobody had to ask any questions.'

Since we do have these distinctions, it is important to develop the concepts correctly. When our buddha nature is disowned, its projection becomes God, a creator divinity external to ourselves, who has power over us and who has to be appeased or manipulated. This is not only disempowering, it creates a belief-system, something that is not based on direct personal experience. 'Religion' has connotations for most of us associated with a belief-system.

The truth taught by the buddhas is that nothing exists outside of the mind – everything is a projection of mind. There is no external God. 'Buddhism can go with any religion,' Jamgon Kongtrul Rinpoche explained, 'because the Buddhist view doesn't conflict with anybody. Buddhism is not some kind of belief-system. This is *within* ourself. We're talking about our nature,' he emphasized. Dzongsar Khyentse Rinpoche was even more emphatic on this issue. 'Buddhists deny that Buddhism is primarily a religion. I will not say that Buddhism is even a belief. We must try to explain it in a very atheistic way.'

How then are we to understand the exotic, boldly expressive forms in primary colours with many heads, arms, legs, staring into reality with expressions we have never seen before? And why are they holding so many unusual objects: bell and *vajra*, drum, *dharma* wheel, sword, skullcup, *phurba* or dagger, *drigu* or curved knife, and trident with heads impaled?

Vajra Yogini is the colour of flame; she stands on a corpse and holds in the crook of her arm a staff adorned with heads in different stages of decay. In one hand is a skullcup brimming with blood, in the other a curved knife poised to strike. Apart from a few strands of bone ornaments, she is naked, dancing with one leg raised in the centre of a circle of flames. Her mouth is slightly open; her eye-teeth protrude on to her lower lip. Her hair is wild, standing electrified on end. She has the curvaceous body of a sixteen-year-old; but in her eyes – if we dare to look directly – the fire of lust has burned and been transformed into wisdom-awareness. Her three eyes stare beyond the temporal into absolute reality. The first Western scholars, about a hundred years ago, projected their own theistic conditioning and concluded that they were witnessing a pantheon of divinities, a corrupt paganistic reversion from the simplicity of the 'monotheistic' serene sitting Buddha. They called it 'Lamaism', a cult of Tibetan priests.

The truth, though, is that these forms are the projections of our own purified, refined senses from the truth dimension known as *sambhogakaya*. At the first stage of enlightenment, known as the first bodhisattva level, the *sambhogakaya* manifests; and these forms appear naturally from the clarity aspect of the mind. 'The *sambhogakaya* is not treated as God,' Gyaltsap Rinpoche explained. 'It is a state of ultimate nature. For the *sambhogakaya* to appear to us, we have to accumulate merit. For those who have enough merit and who have purified themselves enough, the *sambhogakaya* will appear.'

Sambhogakaya is a Sanskrit word. Translated into Tibetan, it means someone who had accomplished all wealth, which refers to everything – all phenomena, every aspect of the truth, so that nothing is lacking. At the same time there is an active awareness, a spontaneous non-stop ability. *Sambhogakaya* describes being-as-quality, potentiality, clarity. So the deities are the forms of our inherent buddha patterns, adorned with the wealth of supreme accomplishment to show the activity of liberation. The ultimate result is not a poor state. It is a state of complete enjoyment, complete wealth – direct, unequivocal, fearless.

Because these forms are deep within our psyche, our awakened nature, they appear for everyone spontaneously at the time right after death, called the *bardo* or intermediary stage between death and rebirth. The gross senses die with the physical body, but after death there are the very subtle, refined senses. Death is actually a very refined part of life. So the *projection* of the refined senses is also much more subtle, and very pure. It is this projection of the refined senses that we call the deity, and these forms will manifest for everyone; every being with buddha nature will see them clearly in the *bardo*.

That is why it is important to work with these forms, recognize them as the enlightened patterns of purified mind, and make them emerge now. When they appear after death, there will be recognition, and like a child meeting its mother, the created and uncreated come together, merging. That is the moment of enlightenment.

If we have not recognized them as the pure patterns of our own mind, there will be tremendous fear, a turning away from the light. Then all the terrors of the mind open; the projections speed up, vivid and threatening, until, blown by the winds of karma and the overwhelming desire to 'substantiate' our existence, we enter a new womb: animal, human, god; or take spontaneous rebirth in the hells of ghost realms. So owning the forms of our buddha nature is not an inconsequential psychological game. More than a matter of life and death, it is a case of complete freedom or continued enslavement. It is urgent, the most important thing we can do.

These forms are the enlightened expression of our buddha nature. Their variety and wealth of display refer to the different patterns our own energy takes. Just as we are all born into a family, and in that family there are certain characteristics, so there is within the mind of each of us a particular buddha family. There are five families of the Buddha, each embodying a different aspect of wisdom, holding particular objects that signify their activity or the skilful means used to liberate beings. Each buddha also fits a pattern of energy in the phenomenal world, corresponding to a colour, a direction, an element; and because our body is a microcosm of the outer phenomenal world, there is a further correspondence with a chakra or subtle nerve centre. On a psychological level, each buddha refers to an aggregate – form, sensation, perception, consciousness and mental activity – the components through which we piece together our version of reality. The end of the line is emotional confusion, which is expressed negatively as ignorance, anger, passion, pride or jealousy.

That tight knot of emotional confusion and the aggregate from which it comes is our working basis; the truth is found where it hurts. The source of suffering is the starting point of wisdom. Habitual patterns – karmic tendencies – are purified by meditating on the pure forms of the wisdom-beings, the *yidams*, who are the enlightened members of the different buddha families. The ultimate result is the appearance of the buddhas. When the five elements have been completely refined, their consorts – the female buddhas – appear. So the buddha families describe, layer by layer from the mental seed to its full maturation in the panoramic display of appearances, the whole gigantic operational interaction between mind and phenomena; a psychological *mappa mundi* with pristine mind at the centre transformed into a particular buddha.

We need somehow to relate more vividly with the buddha families, get to know ourselves through them. Vairochana is white, holds a *dharma* wheel in his right hand and a bell with a wheel on the handle in his left; the *dharma* wheel is the spiritual equivalent of a sceptre – it shows all-pervading rule. The position he occupies is the centre, the element is space. On the impure level this is a person who is clouded by ignorance or stupidity, who has a habit of ignoring anything that is too demanding, too theatening to 'the low-level stability created by ego' as Chogyam Trungpa describes it. It corresponds on a psychological level with the aggregate of form which is purified through the crown chakra into *dharmadhatu* wisdom – the wisdom of seeing things as they actually are.

Akshobya Buddha is blue, holding a *vajra* in his right hand and a bell with *vajra* on the handle in his left. In the phenomenal world, it is the east and the element is water. A *vajra* family person is dominated by the glacial tightness of hatred or anger which links psychologically with the aggregate of consciousness. But that frozen hardness can be purified through the heart chakra to become fluid, reflective. In its supremely distilled form it becomes mirror-like wisdom – the wisdom of seeing as many things as there are in one instant.

Ratnasambhava is yellow and holds a jewel in his right hand and a bell with a jewel on the handle in his left. The element is earth, the direction is south. A *ratna* family person expresses the neurotic energy of pride or arrogance connected psychologically with the aggregate of sensation. It is a fear of not being substantial enough, a need to build things up. But the enriching qualities are inherently there – lushness, expansiveness, generosity. The restriction is purified at the navel chakra expanding into the wisdom of equanimity or equality – seeing without concepts of good or bad.

Amitabha is red, representing the lotus family, and holds a lotus in one hand and a bell with a lotus on the handle in the other. In the phenomenal world it is west, and the element is fire. There is an image here of the setting sun receding into the horizon in a blaze of colour, its burning heat transmuted into pure display. A lotus family person relates through the fire of passion, consuming or appropriating the space of otherness, just like fire. Psychologically it relates to the aggregate of perception. Passion is purified at the throat chakra into the warmth of compassion, and the result is discriminating wisdom, which sees all the particulars of a being in the correct perspective.

Amoghasiddhi is green, holding a double *vajra* in one hand and a bell with a double *vajra* on the handle in the other. It is associated with the north and the element of air. A karma family person is dominated by jealousy or envy, connected with the aggregate of mental activity. It can be expressed as intellectual curiosity, or negatively as snooping around, like the wind prying into all nooks and crannies. When that same energy is liberated from ego, it becomes all-accomplishing wisdom – the ability to perform all activities, to do all that needs to be done.

Buddha activities are separated into four groups, which cover the full range of possibilities: pacifying, enriching, magnetizing or subjugating, and destroying. Each object that the deities hold corresponds to one of these four groups of activity.

Recognizing the buddha family that we belong to is like a flash of awareness. In fact it takes a lot of effort and a long time to return to the family of origin. The guides that lead us home are called *yidams*. They are the enlightened members of the different buddha families. For every neurotic psychological state there is the corresponding *yidam* who enacts its inherent wisdom, holding ritual objects that show the path to liberation. The kinds of energy they express can be peaceful, wrathful or semi-wrathful/ecstatic.

Vajrasattva is white and sits cross-legged in meditation posture, holding a bell in one hand, a *vajra* in the other. His rainbow-coloured robes float like clouds around him. A gentle smile seems to arise from the depths of purity and is reflected on to his serene countenance. He holds his bell gracefully, perhaps even seductively, and we can almost hear it calling us in the still pastel sky.

Vajra Yogini is an example of a semi-wrathful *yidam*, and is graphically depicted in union with her consort, Cakrasamvara. Cakrasamvara has twelve arms, is dark blue and holds a variety of ritual objects, including a bell and *dorje*, a skullcup, a curved knife and a trident with skulls impaled. His feet stand astride two corpses while Vajra Yogini's legs encircle him in a state of being called *mahasukkha*, great bliss – the union of wisdom and compassion, emptiness and skilful means, which is the enlightened state.

The wrathful deities – for example, Vajrakilaya – enact the enormous power of cosmic rage, a primal anger without hatred, which cuts through doubts – like not believing in one's buddha nature – confusions, and all the turbulence of this increasingly dark age. Their mouths are open, fangs bared in a primordial scream so ferocious it is like an electric shock. But in the huge round orbs of their eyes there is stillness, the small quiet space of compassion. They are black and wear bone ornaments and tiger or leopard skins, treading on the corpse of ego. In their hands they hold cutting objects – the *drigu* or curved knife, the *phurba* or three-sided dagger, and the *katvanga* or trident impaled with skulls. Because we have more negative than positive energy, these wrathful forms are a truer representation of the Buddha for these times.

The question is, do we recognize the truth that these wisdom-beings present? Can we cut cleanly through our confusion and identify with these expressions of pure energy? Identification with the *yidam* has to be so complete, we lose the sense of 'I'. 'Instead of simply *negating* the notion of "I" as a fixed, solid entity,' Jamgon Kongtrul Rinpoche explained, 'we visualize ourselves as the deity. So to visualize oneself as the *yidam*, to have the confidence of the *yidam*, we have to let go of clinging to our self.'

The visualization of the *yidam* should be transparent, like a rainbow, and free from fixation – which makes everything solid. The transparency of pure form destroys the karmic tendency to cling to our own solid flesh and blood body, and with it the notion of 'I' – separate, substantial, permanent. By imposing transparency on to solidity, fluidity on to fixation, evanescence on to permanence, old patterns are liberated. Identifying in this way with the *yidam* establishes another kind of karmic tendency; and this leads to awakening from the dream of ignorance.

The *yidams* all enact the transformation of deep inner psychological realities in this kind of very direct, non-egoistic way. The question is, can we meet the challenge, relate to them directly without distortion or manipulation? If we can acknowledge them in this way, we can be transformed using them as guides, to lead us to the family we really belong to.

There is no cultural context here. The forms of the *yidams* may look exotic to us, as though they were produced by an Eastern culture. But they were not produced by any culture at all. 'These *yidam* forms have nothing to do with Tibetan customs,' Jamgon Kongtrul said emphatically. 'These different forms and ornaments have a significance which comes completely from the omniscient wisdom of the Buddha.' That cryptic phrase, 'the wisdom of the Buddha', may sound somewhat theistic, as though there was a doer, some kind of intentionality hard at work behind the scenes. But it simply means the true nature of everything – reality, phenomena, mind; there is no conflict, because the true nature of everything is emptiness, from which anything can manifest. And these forms are what emerge at the purest, deepest level of mind.

In the Vajrayana, the means whereby this level is uncovered is shown by the ritual objects that the *yidams* hold. 'Ritual objects are the *exact* method,' Jamgon Kongtrul explained. They are symbols of the transformation process, charged with esoteric meaning. 'Just showing the symbols and signs,' Gyaltsap Rinpoche commented, 'can bring a lot of benefit for beings. Because of that, they hold different kinds of ritual objects.' Focusing on them while visualizing the deity can give birth to deeper understanding.

Foremost in significance of all the ritual objects are the bell and the *vajra*, which contain a wealth of esoteric meaning that points out the entire Vajrayana path, and together describe the union of male (*vajra*) and female (bell), or method and wisdom in the state of enlightenment. They are 'original' esoteric symbols from the womb of origination, appearing together with the form of the primordial Buddha as the signs of attainment of ultimate wisdom. 'The origin of the bell and *vajra*,' Gyaltsap Rinpoche revealed, 'is that the primordial Buddha Vajradhara had a bell and *vajra* in his hand which was produced through the perfection of wisdom. The realization of ultimate truth matured as these two symbols.' That is their hidden meaning, the source of their wealth.

On the neck of the bell there is the face of Vairochana, the Buddha of form, which means that the bell is the body representation of the Buddha. The line of small *vajras* circling the base of the bell signifies the protective enclosure drawn round the perimeter of every sacred space. On the dome of the bell is inscribed an eight-petal lotus, the residence of the deity, or buddha palace. Inside each petal are four syllables in the four directions representing the consorts of the different buddha families; the syllable *lam* which represents the consort of Vairochana, has to face its partner, the head of the Buddha. In the four intermediate directions are the seed syllables of the *dakinis* or female *yidams* of the buddha families. The five-pronged *vajra* which crowns the handle represents the five wisdoms of the buddha families.

So the bell shows all the female qualities of enlightenment. It is hollow, empty, but in that space there is quality or potentiality, which is sound; pure manifestation which takes the form of the lotus, the palace of the female buddhas or *dakinis*, with the form buddha topmost and central, wearing a crown of the five wisdoms. The enlightened female mandala shows that emptiness is form, and form emptiness; that they are interwoven. This is the essence of the Buddha's teaching on transcendent wisdom, or *prajnaparamita*, given at Vulture's Peak in the historic second turning of the wheel. The embodiment of highest wisdom, the bell is saying, is quintessentially female.

The bell is the body of the Buddha, and the sound it makes is his speech. So the *vajra* represents buddha mind, again with a tremendous wealth of esoteric meaning. The formation of the *vajra* is five prongs on either side of a round centre and eight petals below each set of prongs. The round centre is the womb of origin, again pointing to the heart of the Buddha's teaching on the indivisibility of appearance and emptiness. The eight petals of the lotus on either side refer to the pure forms of appearance in a more active aspect: the eight bodhisattvas and their consorts. These bodhisattvas are the forms that arise naturally from the purification of the sense consciousnesses: hearing, smelling, seeing, tasting, consciousness of body and of mind, the ground consciousness where all tendencies are stored, and the *klesa* consciousness which holds the basic obscuring patterns of ego-clinging.

The five upper prongs of the *vajra* show the five buddhas; the lower five, their consorts. In its impure state, the five buddhas are, as we have seen, the five aggregates, and their consorts are the five elements. So the *vajra* shows the activity aspect of liberation; in a word it is spiritual accomplishment. When Guru Rinpoche subdued the demonic forces in Tibet, he held his *vajra* in the *mudra* or gesture of subjugation.

The bell and *vajra* are a primordial couple, inseparable in meaning. The bell is emptiness: the womb, the residence, the container. The *vajra* is activity, method, expression. It shows the skilful means of the path — exactly how to get there. Their union is enlightenment.

All ritual objects have a similar profound meaning. The three points of Guru Rinpoche's *katvanga* show his ability to destroy the three mind poisons of all beings: ignorance, aggression and passion. Below the cross-blades of the trident, there are three heads: a skull, a dried head and a freshly severed head, pointing to the three reflexes or bodies of the Buddha. The multi-coloured double *vajra* on the *katvanga* shows his mastery of the four kinds of activity — increasing, pacifying, magnetizing and destroying. Tied on to the *katvanga* are white ribbons flowing in the wind, showing his ability to help beings on any of the paths. In his left hand is a skullcup filled with the nectar of immortality; and in the skullcup is the vase of deathless life, the sign of having attained immortality.

When the great Indian *mahasiddha* Tilopa was training his disciple Naropa, he pointed to different symbols of the ultimate truth, through which Naropa understood the meaning of authentic reality without the interpretive medium of words. Some of these symbols were very mundane, not even slightly esoteric; but because the thread of enlightenment is continuous or inherent in everything, Tilopa could imbue them with profound significance.

It is this kind of profound meaning that ritual objects contain: pointing to the hidden meaning underlying apparent phenomena. 'All these objects,' Gyaltsap Rinpoche emphasized, 'have appeared as the perfection of the primordial Buddha Vajradhara. Their origin should be treated from the ultimate realization of the perfection of wisdom. We cannot point to the particular date when such and such an object was invented, discovered or created because all these things *appeared*; they were not created.

'So since there is no beginning of the *kalpa*, from beginningless time therefore, all these ritual objects are already there in the ultimate sphere. We cannot point to any beginning.'

II. MAKING IT EMERGE

Historically, the beginning of Vajrayana ritual can be traced very clearly to the fourth turning of the wheel: the Tantric teachings of the Buddha. In the first turning of the wheel, at the Deer Park in Sarnath, the Buddha taught conduct, or morality; in the second turning, at Vulture's Peak, wisdom; in the third, meditation and clarity. These are all called sutra teachings, discourses spoken by the Buddha. After that, in what is sometimes called the fourth turning, the Buddha transformed himself into the primordial Buddha Vajradhara and emanated the form of the *yidam* at the centre of the mandala to teach the *tantras* to the most advanced disciples. But this transformation was visible only to those beings karmically mature enough to benefit from them. So from the very beginning the *tantras* were highy esoteric. They were, in fact, revelation.

The *tantras* were recorded, and when the *dharma* reached Tibet in the eighth century, they were translated in the great collection of all the Buddha's teachings known as the Kangyur. Commentaries on them by the great scholars and *mahasiddhas* of the seventh century were compiled in the Tangyur. The *tantras* explain all the aspects of ritual, and it is this tradition which has been followed precisely in Vajrayana practice to the present day. They describe the various instruments to be used; where to play music; how to arrange the various types of offerings on the shrine; how to use the ritual vase or *boompa*; how to make the *damaru* – the small hand drum – and bell, and how to keep them properly; how to use the *phurba* or ritual dagger.

The short *tantra* of Cakrasamvara explains the importance of using bell, drum, cymbals and flute. Imagining all the harmonious sounds throughout the universe all gathered together and offered to the buddhas, it is said, brings such wealth of merit that one will gain power over all the great deities. So the purpose of music is to make the most exalted offering to the buddhas, creating in the spirit of inspiration the vast accumulation of merit which gives birth to enlightened mind.

All music in Tantric ritual is inspired and passed on through 'received' experience: instruction in visions by the different deities to the great masters. Quite recently, Tenga Rinpoche, one of the foremost Vajrayana ritual masters, witnessed the occasion of a new piece of visionary music.

'One morning, while I was staying at Rumtek Monastery, the Karmapa called for two jaling players to come very quickly. When they arrived, he instructed them to play a piece of music he had just received in a visionary experience. He was told that if this music was played, the *dharma* of the Buddha would spread; and that the music should be called "Victory Banner of the *Dharma*."

'There's another piece of music,' he continued, 'called the "Glorious Copper Coloured Mountain". It originated when the 6th Karmapa had the experience of going to the Copper-Coloured Mountain and receiving empowerments and instruction from Guru Rinpoche. He heard music there, remembered it, and taught it to his disciples. There are many kinds of music like that,' he reflected, 'and all come from the visionary experiences of the lamas. None of it is "composed".'

The entire Vajrayana is an empowered container enhancing everything that is already there, purifying and refining it skilfully till dross becomes gold. It works on all levels, from outer offerings to the subtlest of mental patterns. The great kings of India and Tibet used their wealth to make sumptuous ritual offerings. Powdered lapis was used for drawing the mandala, intricate gold carvings adorned musical instruments. But the simple yogis and *mahasiddhas* living in caves used clay and sand. 'Actually, there's no difference,' Gyaltsap Rinpoche commented, 'whether we use an instrument made from precious objects or not. There's no difference between ordinary substance and very precious things. The important thing is to offer it to the buddhas with our mind.'

To bring out pure perception all the patterns of ordinary daily life are used in Tantric ritual. Just as we invite our guests to visit us, offer them something to eat, and praise their good qualities, so we invite the *yidams*, invoking their presence through music and prayer, making offerings to them and requesting them to remain. 'Vajrayana is very skilful means,' Jamgon Kongtrul explained, 'because it works, it fits together with everyday life. A lot of people think there is no connection between Vajrayana ritual and all the other activities. But this is wrong. If we understand it correctly, every movement, every moment, whatever we do, has a connection with everything else.' Vajrayana ritual is like an inspired blueprint placed on top of gross habitual patterns, elevating them to a very high frequency.

That continuum brings about a natural classification into four or five types of buddha activity. Dzongsar Khyentse Rinpoche explained precisely how the types of activity are harnessed skilfully for the purpose of realization through ritual. 'Buddha has five different manifestations – five *dakinis*, five colours, five elements and five actions: pacifying, enriching, magnetizing, destroying, and supreme, which is the unity of the four others. There's no action possible other than these, scientifically speaking, even in ordinary life. There are only those five and they are the display of the energy of buddha nature, which is the source of the buddhas of the five families. These energies exist within oneself.

'In order to reach or realize buddha nature,' he continued, 'we do many different things. Most of the time we do pacifying meditation, to pacify the emotions. Most meditation is in this category; within it is contained all the other activities, like pacifying-enriching, pacifying-magnetizing, even pacifying-wrathful, in which we put all our negative emotions under the earth, suppressing them.

'Pacifying and purifying are connected,' he explained. 'Pacifying means rejecting, and by that rejection, getting something. For example, automatically we get clean clothes as you wash away the dirt – so washing is a rejection of the dirt. We use many different methods – love and compassion, for example. Pacifying is usually emphasized because it is the best: it is safe, harmless, and if you are good at that, then through pacifying you can do all the other activities.

'The other activities are quite dangerous for humans,' he warned. 'Instead of actually getting there, they may wander. Enriching, magnetizing and wrathful activities – if you are good at these...' He paused.

'It's a deviation?' I suggested.

'Yes, we should do all these to realize the unity of *sambhogakaya* and *dharmakaya*'; to realize buddha nature, in other words, rather than getting side-tracked with the powerful vehicle that's taking us there.

'For magnetizing energy, we need to create lots of atmosphere,' he continued, 'Like red flowers and red clothes, wine – which is an intoxicating and seducing substance – warmth, things like that. Some yogis and yoginis do it to magnetize their consorts.'

Wrathful rituals actually create the energy of warfare, using the clashing sound of special cymbals – the *rolmo* – with offerings made to look like weapons, and the *phurba* or dagger to destroy negativity. The most spectacular one happens regularly on the last day of the year. The colourful finale of an elaborate week-long ritual of sacred dance and prayers occurs when negative energy 'trapped' within a network of coloured string is set ablaze in preparation for the New Year. 'This is warfare activity,' Dzongsar Khyentse commented, 'belonging to the wrathful category of buddha activity.'

Prosperity activity has to do with spreading, increasing or expanding, making things multiply. To activate that kind of energy, auspiciousness is important – quite simply, being in the right place at the right time. It is involved with a particular quality known as *yang*, which can be described briefly as enriching and magnetizing power, or presence in a charismatic sense; an ability to magnetize what is needed. 'This kind of enriching energy exists within oneself,' Dzongsar Khyentse explained. 'What we do [in ritual] is depend on the circumstances, situation and substance, and *make it emerge*.'

The early Vajrayana Buddhists in Tibet took the idea of *yang* from the old shamanistic Bon religion, and put it into the buddha activity of enrichment or prosperity, in the family of Ratnasambhava. The symbol is the jewel, the colour is yellow, the direction is south, and the deities invoked are Dzamballa or Pravati. *Yang* ritual magnetizes this quality through prayer, visualization and meditation, purifying the lack of *yang*, then enriching and storing it. Although it often has a wordly aspect, possessing *yang* assists in realizing buddha nature because it provides a healthy environment for growth – material and spiritual.

Perhaps I should confess here and now that I have a great appreciation of *yang* quality, having experienced very extreme points in life when nothing would come my way, or stay when it did. I understand now what this elusive energy is that makes us become successful, prosperous and flourishing. Tai Situpa described it with an image: '*Yang* is like a mountain with a beautiful lake in front. It is wealth, richness, not necessarily money, but richness. I think that Van Gogh's painting "Sunflower," though it is just oil and canvas, has a quality. I would call that quality *yang*.'

The reason it is so important to be aware of this concept is that we all have it, but there are ways of increasing as well as decreasing it, and it has primarily to do with conduct. Respecting and using everything for what it is meant for, is a simple way to describe how to increase *yang*. It means acknowledging an inherent order, respecting the relative world. Dressing appropriately and carrying oneself properly create an elegance; and elegance is a *yang* quality. Respecting one's environment means putting everything in the right place: sacred images and texts on a shrine, not the floor. Misusing the Buddha as a doorstop or lampstand will certainly decrease *yang*. Mindfulness in conduct creates impeccability, and that is a *yang* quality.

'Any kind of misconduct will definitely destroy it,' Tai Situpa emphasized. So all the injunctions of the universal moral order apply: deviant sexuality, drug abuse, lying, stealing, killing, alcoholism, violence. Even dressing inappropriately will decrease *yang*. 'I definitely think that if you have new clothes and then make a hole in them on purpose and wear them, it's not good for *yang*,' Tai Situpa explained. 'In England, the punks have no *yang*, nor do the younger generation of Germans – very little *yang*.' When traditions are not respected and eventually lost, or when traditional cultures are destroyed in times of social upheaval, the universal *yang* goes down. Our circumstances become impoverished; quite simply, there is no growth.'

So, getting back to ritual, sacred objects, and buddha activity, when prosperity ritual is performed, the *yang* may be stored in a special object, which then contains *yang* energy. Beru Khyentse Rinpoche revealed how a very special *dakini's kapala* or skullcup came to him. 'A few hundred years ago, there was a family living in the area round Tsari Mountain, a famous sacred place in Tibet, who came by a *dakini's kapala*. These are very thin, like eggshell, and when you look through them, you can see the light – which is a very good sign. They are usually small, light, and a pleasing shape, with all the signs inside. Sometimes they are found open, rather than upside down, and filled with flowers. Another good sign is that there is some kind of light coming from it at night. Even if you try to find one, you cannot get it; it just has to come your way.

'There was a family feud and the head of the family, who was very attached to this *kapala*, feared that one day it would be stolen. So he offered it to me, and I kept it. Because he'd asked different lamas to perform *yangdrup* – *yang*-increasing prayers, or merit – with it, the *kapala* contained his *yang*. I've found that since I've had this *kapala*, everything is just coming to me without having to look for it.

'One of my monks also found a special *kapala*,' he added. 'He was very happy about it and kept it carefully. One day he looked for it and it was gone. Who had taken it, he didn't know; but it was lost, gone.'

No one can possess and keep a sacred object unless it belongs to him inherently. In the true sense of ownership, nothing can be possessed that does not belong, and nothing that belongs can really be lost. It is this kind of inherent wealth that resides within our buddha nature. It is the ultimate *yang* in a sense, and when that vast natural resource is opened, developed, the outer forms of wealth manifest.'

I was intrigued by the implications. 'When a master obtains a sacred object,' I asked Tai Situpa, 'is it possible it can contain his *yang*?'

'Sometimes. Yes, sometimes.'

'And if he loses it, then his personal power might diminish?'

'Possibly.'

'So in that sense, the more sacred objects a master has, the greater his power and ability to perform buddha activity?'

'Yes,' he agreed, 'I think so.' He paused a moment. 'Rather materialistic, isn't it?' he said laughing.

I shook my head. The profound meaning of buddha activity seemed awesome suddenly. I felt a kind of stillness going deeper and deeper, like an anchor dropping into the ocean. 'I think it's very special, really quite wonderful.'

So wonderful, it may be forgotten what these messengers of the buddhas are really for. Sacred objects – whether they are *rangjung* or created, whether they are *terma* or from another realm – the basic principle is the same. As Jamgon Kongtrul said 'They're all skilful means for liberating beings.' The blessing power of the buddhas.

PART II

The Hidden Lands of Padmasambhava:

Gateway to Wisdom Mind

VII

○

Journey to the Heart of Light

In 1981 during the seven-week period of ceremonies marking the *parinirvana* (passing into enlightenment) of the 16th Karmapa, I journeyed into West Sikkim on pilgrimage. It was late November, with bright, sun-filled days and cold, bone-biting nights, when I started walking from Pemayangtse, an important Nyingmapa monastery, to the mountaintop hermitage of Tashiding, the foremost sacred site in Sikkim. At that time there was no direct road linking the sites *en route* in a circle – clockwise circumambulation or *korra* describes the movement of the pilgrim – so in many places I ventured along the rim of mountains on foot-sized goat trails into the untouched garden paradise of Sikkim; through fragrant cardamon forests into sunlit orange groves, crossing a river over a swaying, frayed rope bridge, to a lake set deep in the midst of an ancient forest, so utterly tranquil it seemed enchanted. It was Khechuperi, a lake blessed by Padmasambhava. At another place near a river where hot sulphur springs formed huge healing tubs, there was an opening into the rocks. A small entranceway like a porch led into a great cavern where a natural skylight threw a shaft of light on to an unmistakeable outline – the enormous bodyprint of Guru Padmasambhava.

Sikkim is radiant with natural wonders like that. The pilgrimage gradually became an inner experience of clarity and light inseparable from the spacious luminosity of the blue sky, the brilliance of the sun, the cascading chutes of water forming icy pools into which I plunged, the texture of the soil that gave life to flowers and fruit. Unknowingly, I had stepped inside a sacred circle, one of the major hidden lands of Padmasambhava, concealed like a treasure to be opened at the right time. Even less did I realize that the pinpoints of clarity I felt were the faintest glimpses of the inner hidden land – the level of pure perception that is the real destination of every pilgrim.

When the elements of the outer environment are in harmony, the individual body is attuned. That is the gateway to wisdom mind. My pilgrimage continued eleven years later when I asked Tai Situpa, at his monastery in northern India, to tell me about the *beyul*, as the hidden lands are known in Tibetan. His guidance was simple and clear. 'Beyul is by definition places that are yet to be discovered, hidden until the appropriate time for discovery is reached. These places have various potentials to offer. Some are specifically beneficial during the time of famine and war; some are very particular to the time when people need spiritual inspiration, spiritual benefit. These are special places for quicker realization, having a more appropriate and powerful environment for inner development. When the environment is in harmony, then it will make a person physically in harmony, and that makes mental harmony.'

The Prophecies of Padmasambhava describe the great cycles of change that will occur in the environment and this is the background for the hidden lands. 'Know that all composite phenomena are impermanent,' begins Padmasambhava, addressing an assembly of disciples in eighth-century Tibet.

> Now is the lucky period without misfortune, for we have a collection of [good] conditions of the outer and inner habitat and inhabitants. It is a period during which the elements of the external world are in harmony, with a balanced season of heat, moisture, warmth, production and growth. The gods of the elements prosper and assist the inhabitants. There is timely monsoon, crops and ever excellent livestock. Rich flora and fauna beautify the nine regions of Tibet. The mountains, rocks and caves stand solid in their original position... The sun, moon, stars and time are not erratic.
>
> Tibet in general enjoys a glorious prosperity, endowed with flowers and lakes. Her people ... enjoy long life free from sickness and excellent resources. People are comely like the divine parents ... all speech is articulate, fluent and pleasant. People are not impatient, nor do they use impolite speech through the force of the five poisonous delusions. They live skilfully in peace, harmony and friendship, spending day and night in tender fondness according to *dharma*; find food, drink, clothes and ornaments effortlessly, and abide by the law combining human and divine principles...
>
> The four legged animals find plenty of pasture and water ... Their product is bountiful and nutritious like that of our mothers.

The golden age of harmony reigned in Tibet twelve hundred years ago. Our own golden age lies buried in a mythological past; in Tibet it is merely history. There the perfect balance of life and the environment – the 'inner and outer habitat' – was upheld by the strict moral principles of Buddhist law. 'Buddhism is flourishing and the law is strict,' Padma explains. 'The traditions of monastic rules and discourses are firmly established.' This foundation of moral precepts gives rise to the fruits of meditation. 'There are many realized meditators,' he confirms. 'The power of devotees, men or women, is so strong that they even honour the dust under the soles of the shoes of their masters . . . All are self-disciplined and uphold their own spiritual tradition.'

Society as a whole is balanced with a wise leadership in harmony with the *dharma*.

> The King's command is absolute and luminating with the light of compassion. The objectives of ministers are honest and candid in congruence with the *dharma*. Basically, the subjects enjoy the pleasures of *samsara*: nuns are wise . . . the social prestige and dignity is weighty, the royal sons are jubilant, conscientious, attractive . . .

'Such a state of happiness is similar to Tushita heaven,' the passage concludes lyrically.

'However,' the great Guru warned prophetically, 'this world is impermanent like a city of illusion. It will not last long but is subject to destruction and change.' There is no God-like judgement, no pronouncement of just punishment for righteous cause; just a description of the inevitability of change. 'Good or bad, day or night are all alike, for the cycle of rise and fall is like summer, spring, autumn and winter. Because of the force of outer natural conflicts of elements, many natural catastrophes will occur.'

> Finally, during the end of this decadent age, fire will fail and create imbalance of heat and cold; water will fail and transmute wet and dry; earth will fail and hurl, destroy or shake; wind will fail and cause undue wavering; space will fail and reveal many different colours. As a consequence the forces of elements will become erratic in various ways, and reveal evil omens and miracles: roaring of thunder, lightning, hail, storms and hurricane, as well as of breaking glaciers, cracking earth, and of tumbling rocks and hills which will shake the earth, stir volcanoes and destroy crops.

He could be describing our own diseased ecosystem.

> Years, months, seasons, sun, moon, planets and stars will deviate. The earth will lose its fertility and the forests will dry up. Vegetation, dairy

products and honey will lack essential nutrition. The lustre of the surroundings will wane and hurricanes of red dust will blow. Unclean and misty smoke will billow the sky...

The economy is equally bankrupt. 'Treasuries speculated will be gradually emptied.' The same applies to spiritual artefacts.

> Temples and objects of worship built inside or outside will be demolished by natural catastrophe or fire and water... Insects, worms and birds will wander around and infest images whose bodies and heads are dislocated... ritual articles will be burned, abandoned underground and become the objects of destruction and robbery. Similar will also be the texts of teachings. The pages of manuscripts will be found winnowed by wind in empty ruins... Animals such as wild ass, bear and ogress will wander in the holy places. The *stupas* will be dug and their contents stolen...

The effect on humankind is demoralizing. 'The teachings in general shall wane, and so shall I, their servant,' Padma predicts, showing the dependency of the teachings on the outer and inner environment.

Because of the natural laws of interdependence, when nature is agitated, 'the merits of the common and monastic community will gradually deteriorate. The law of the king will break as when a glacier is hit by lightning... Like the breaking of a pool, the teachings of Sakyamuni will gradually vanish and finally be enshrouded in darkness.' When this happens, 'the water of blessing will dry up,' and 'those who sincerely practise will be as rare as a star in broad daylight'. Accordingly, 'the merits and energy of all practitioners will become weak, their life cut short... [the common] people will lack lustre and stink enshrouded in dust, ugly, lacking faith and will indulge in devilish acts. Their life will be short and most will die untimely.'

The root cause of this enormous upheaval is clear: 'There will be an extremely unbalanced environment due to the disturbance of the elements,' Padma emphasized. And again, 'The disturbance caused by the elements will be beyond words.'

The text describes five kinds of extreme disturbance: the Dregs of Sickness when all kinds of illness never before heard of will spread; the Dregs of Weapons when great wars will break out and people kill each other; the Dregs of Famine when crops fail and many die of hunger; the Dregs of the Disturbance of the Fundamental Elements, when 'the function of elements such as fire, water and wind will become unbalanced and huge mountains and valleys will make the environment unpleasant'; and for the Tibetan people in particular, the Dregs of the Black Devils, when the barbarian Mongols will wage war on their neighbours. The collapse of the outer environment gives rise to the Five Dregs, and the last one especially, is an ominous portent for the whole world.

> The law of Tibet will break. Chinese, Mongols and the barbarians of the borderland will wage war. There will be mass fighting and killings; an ocean of blood will be formed. The land will be filled with skeletons ... In general the whole world will change as if a great hurricane had blown in the ocean. In particular the whole nation of the Snow Land will be agitated by war.

During this time when 'even the minds of the bodhisattvas will become disturbed', 'all those with good karma and practitioners of the *dharma* will escape to borderlands'. In the last instance, 'those who preserve and disseminate the doctrine will withdraw their activities and travel to the heavens'.

Seeing the momentous cycles of change in the environment that would afflict practitioners of *dharma* in the future, the great Guru sanctified 108 remote valleys – the hidden lands – throughout the Himalayas, composed detailed guidebooks to their location, and concealed them as *terma* texts. 'Some of these *beyul* are in the depths of the jungle,' Tai Situpa commented, 'some are in the midst of the snow mountains. All of them, somehow, are very hard to reach; but when the appropriate time approaches, they will be reached. There will be a particular person or persons who will unveil them.' Here begins the mythological journey to the heart of light, the quest for ultimate wisdom in which the outer environment mirrors the inner journey.

A similar natural process guides me to people with a personal story of the hidden lands to tell. It is the power of surrender that activates the inner guide and opens a flow of energy that has nothing to do with the will. I was having a sober conversation about the hidden land of Pemako with Karma Thinley Rinpoche at his monastery in Nepal when a woman's voice interrupted suddenly. 'In May, June and July the snow melts and then you can go to *beyul* Pemako,' the voice said with authority. 'In winter, spring and autumn it's all sealed by snow and then nobody can go.'

I looked around to see an old Tibetan nun speaking confidently about her personal experience. Her words were riveting. 'The birds there sing the Guru Rinpoche mantra.' Her voice became high and light. '*Om Ah Hung Bendza Guru Pema Siddhi Hung*', she sang. 'There's milky water and *tsampa* [barley porridge] made by trees that you can eat.' She laughed with delight, like a child.

Hearing these words from her own experience acted like a transmission, a vivid flash of insight into another dimension. It was the difference between looking at a map and seeing a moving picture of a place with live people in it. I began to understand the hidden lands as real places that fortunate people could enter, not as poignant reminders of humanity's eternal utopian quest to regain a lost paradise. Themes as ancient as the dawn of consciousness were there, but with this vivid transmission there was flesh on the bones.

Recurrent images of all allegorical journeys became a living reality: a guide who had a dream or vision indicating that the time was right, and who revealed the guidebook; a dangerous inaccessible route up steep mountains, through dense jungle with poisonous snakes and tigers; ritual offerings to propitiate the guardian deities of the land, especially the female embodiments of wisdom, the *dakinis*; a code of pure moral conduct for the seekers; and caves or lakes within the hidden land with miraculously concealed treasure troves of jewels, food substances, domestic implements, power objects to eliminate obstacles, innermost mind teachings, and the elixir of life. The end of the journey mirrored the abundance of the ultimate limitless attainment – a garden paradise flowing with nutritious milky water, producing food on the bark of trees.

The hidden lands point to the literal truth of the archetypal journey through the outer conscious level, treading on primitive terrain to open up the secret, most inaccessible hidden lands – the formless *dharmakaya*. It is there and present, inside the innermost essence of the mind: the heart chakra centre shaped like an eight-petalled lotus.

An important teaching which pointed out the essence of the hidden lands came through Thinley Norbu Rinpoche. 'The holiest special place,' he revealed, 'is *dharmakaya*. This is Buddha's place. Not everyone can go to this automatically; the only way to get there is through practice... In order to reach *dharmakaya*'s and *sambhogakaya*'s hidden place, we must rely on *nirmanakaya*. So if one has a lot of faith and merit, one can reach the *nirmanakaya* hidden place.' The hidden lands are accessible on the physical dimension, acting as gateways to enlightenment, to the heart of the lotus centre within.

Pemako, as I discovered, means 'lotus display' and spreads from Kham, in eastern Tibet to the province of Arunachel Pradesh in the most north-easterly corner of India. In the early seventeenth century, the *terton* Rigzin Jatson Nyingpo (born 1585) revealed the first guidebook to Pemako, a *terma* text concealed by Padmasambhava. A generation later Rigzin Dudul Dorje (born 1615) also took out a guidebook to Pemako from a rock on the north bank of the Dongcu River. It is said that he opened up or 'clarified in a general way the gateway to the pilgrimage centre of the secret land of Pemako'.[1]

It was not until the late eighteenth century, though, that 'three emanational awareness holders'[2] – Gampopa Orgyen Drodul Lingpa, Rigzin Dorje Thokme and Choling Karwang Chime Dorje – opened up Pemako as a place of pilgrimage.

My auspicious connection with Pemako led me to uncover its recent history. In the late 1950s a group of about thirty Tibetan families planned an escape from the Chinese to the hidden land, but they could not find their way through landslides and dense forest. They returned to Kangpo and there met with the great *terton* Dudjom Rinpoche, who was born in Pemako, and who gave blessing and teaching to some of the group. They decided to send out an advance party of six people to map the route through to Lho Yunden, following the guiding instructions presented by the *terton* Shangling Tubchen.

I found two of the most important members of this group at a bustling two-roomed family dwelling in Bir near Sherabling Monastery in northern India: Lama Setchou and his sister Khandro Tongyang, the consort of the *terton* Pegyal Lingpa – the treasure-finders whose special destiny it was to take out *ter* from Pemako. Khandro Tongyang led me away from the hissing primus stove in the busy kitchen into the peace of her shrine room where a large photograph of Pegyal Lingpa dominated. There, with his sister sitting attentively beside him ready to add details here and there, Lama Setchou recalled his momentous journey to the hidden land accompanied by Pegyal Lingpa. Thirty years before brother and sister had shared the extraordinary experience of living for three years in an unexplored hidden land whose treasures were still sealed. I must have passed their door many times while living at Sherabling, but their story of the hidden land remained concealed till that moment. Lama Setchou began.

'The route to Pemako was so arduous, the Chinese couldn't follow us there,' he explained. 'We had to pass through dense jungle, up and over mountain passes, crossing many rivers where there were leaches. There were snakes – some harmless, some poisonous. The harmless ones had been tamed by Guru Rinpoche, who put a crossed *vajra* on them. There was a mark on their heads, so we knew they were not poisonous. There were also tigers.

'Nearby Pemako there is a region inhabited by the "black Lho", people who are naked, like the inhabitants of Nagaland in India. They kill people and really cause disturbance. They have no *dharma*. Inside Pemako are the "white Lho" who are Buddhist. Almost everyone rises at three in the morning to do some special *dharma* practice. In fact, if a sinner reaches there he won't commit much wrong-doing. You just feel like practising *dharma* once you reach there. The people are very good-natured, very devoted and generous.

'Pemako is called by that name,' he explained, 'because its shape and formation from above is like a lotus. There are many lotus flowers there, and in the rays of the morning sun, they open. The lotus becomes delightful. All around Pemako are mountains and rivers.

'There's a special place there which everyone can see. It's a huge mountain which has many images of buddhas and bodhisattvas. The mountain is shaped like a horse, and in the mouth of the head there's a cave where Padmasambhava meditated for three years. As soon as you enter the cave you are fascinated. There's the feeling you can see lots of Sanskrit letters on the rocks, but when you go closer to the rocks, you can't see anything. Outside the cave you can also see big Mani letters, spontaneously arisen, but when you approach the rocks, the letters are not there. You can read one or two letters, but the rest just disappears.

'Pemako is a very special place,' he continued. 'When you close your eyes and relax, whatever you hear are *dharma* sounds; the birds sing the Guru Rinpoche mantra, "Om Ah Hung Benza Guru Pema Siddhi Hung". When you open your eyes, you just see earth and stones, though. Yes,' he reflected, 'there's something very special about it. Even the animals who eat the grass can make footprints on rock, and the birds too. You can see their footprints on rock as if they had stepped in mud. It's something to do with the grass.'

He paused while I waited expectantly. He had been to a magic land, but like most Tibetans, he was solid as the ground itself, his mind carefully trained to remember precise details. I listened intently. 'There is a story about this. There were two hunters and a dog who went out hunting. It was about to rain. While waiting for some animals to appear, one hunter picked up a blade of grass and started chewing it, as you do sometimes to pass the time. After eating a bit he spat it out, and the dog started licking what he had spat out. It started raining lightly and a white rainbow appeared. Instantly, both the dog and the hunter disappeared, almost as if they had got rainbow body just by eating the grass.'

He continued his reminiscences, touching the heart of the powerful blessing of the hidden lands: the special creative harmony of the outer environment that propels the mind to rest in its natural state — primordial awareness. 'When someone becomes ill in Pemako, before they die a white rainbow appears above the house. When that happens, it means you will die there,' he explained. 'Everyone who goes there attains some realization, just by being there, because it is the holy place of Padmasambhava. Even if a dog dies, a rainbow appears.

'Eighteen people from our party died in Pemako, and before they died we could see rainbows inside their tents — round rainbows. Inside the rainbows we could see different lamas. Those of us who survived thought we were lucky not to have died. But now we realize we were not lucky at all, that we *could* have died there. All those who did attained some realization.

'Pemako is the sacred place of Vajra Yogini.' My heart jumped as he began a description of the inner sacred level. 'And Marme Kumbum,' he continued, 'is the heart of that place. The holiest place of the *dakini* is on the inner part of the lotus, at its very centre. Pegyal Lingpa said he had many *ters* to take from Oden [meaning luminous] Lake within the inner part of Pemako.'

I sat entranced as Lama Setchou offered an eyewitness acount of the thrilling revelation of water treasure. Khandro Tongyang gazed intently into space, the rhythm of her mantra repetitions stilled. A hush came over the room. 'Since Khandro Tongyang is my sister,' he began, 'Pegyal Lingpa explained to me that he had to take a *ter* from the lake, and if I could offer my sister to him as a consort, he would have the necessary *tendrel* to do it. I didn't know if he was serious or not, if he was playing with me or not — he already had one wife. So I replied that if he would take the *ter* in front of everyone as evidence, then I would be ready to give him my sister. Rinpoche agreed to take the *ter* publicly.

'I invited the important people of Pemako, including two *Rinpoches*, one of whom was the Tulku Chogyur Lingpa. We arranged everything and on the full moon day about four or five hundred of the white inhabitants gathered. We pitched tent by the lake, and with all the people and masters made feast offering prayers. We were chanting the mantra of Guru Rinpoche, "*Om Ah Hung Benza Guru Pema Siddhi Hung*", when many rainbows appeared suddenly, on the spot. Immediately Pegyal Lingpa took off his clothes and went into the lake. Everyone was astonished and ran around the lake following him, including myself.

'It was a poisonous lake, so if any people or animals went into it, their whole body would be covered in sores. A short time before, another *terton*, Nangchen Tenga Tulku, had tried to control the spirit of this lake. He thought if he could control it, he would have everything under his control. He went into the lake up to his waist; but he got sores and died. Someone tried to follow Pegyal Lingpa into the water, but he became very afraid: the water started hissing and bubbling till he thought it would overflow. Many people saw fire burning inside the water of the lake, and many of them were frightened.

'With the water spurting up into a fountain, Pegyal Lingpa disappeared underneath, and stayed under for a long time. After half an hour he emerged from the lake. We are not sure how he came out; we just can't remember clearly. But when he came out of the lake he was clutching something in his fist. He asked for a bowl. The two *khandros* – his new and previous wives – brought a bowl. He put what was inside his fist into the bowl. It was a black solid thing. Rinpoche showed it to all the assembled people and gave blessing with it. Inside the black object there was *chokser* [the secret script], *mendrup* [dharma medicine] and the hair of Sri Singha, Manjushrimitra, Garab Dorje and Vimalamitra. This is the first *terma* he took from Pemako,' Lama Setchou concluded, 'and it is called the father *terma*.'

I found out later that Pegyal Lingpa had kept the Pemako *terma* – the Kusum Gongdu – for twenty-four years and then did a three-year retreat to discover the contents of the secret script. In 1987, a year before his death, he gave the reading transmission and empowerment for it – essential rituals to pass on its realization power to others.

'The second *ter* is called the mother *ter*,' Lama Setchou continued. 'Previously, I said that the place on the inner part of the lotus is the heart of the *dakini* Vajra Yogini. Marme Kumbum is at the very centre of the lotus in Pemako. There is a mountain here shaped like a heart, with dense forest, very green meadows and springs of flowing water. It's a very beautiful place. It's from here that the second *terma* was taken.

'Marme Kumbum was one day's walk away. There were seventy or eighty people with us at the time, including Ringaud Tulku. During the day we performed feast-offering prayers. That evening we slept there. Early in the morning while it was still dark, Rinpoche awoke and told all the people to get up, and to get ready immediately. I got up quickly and put on my *shentab* [outer tunic]. Both *khandros* and Rinpoche went first. After the three of them, Ringaud Tulku and I started to walk in the same direction.

'Then Pegyal Lingpa took a hammer and struck a white square-shaped rock the size of a large tent or a small house, some distance away. On the very spot it struck the rock a fire started to burn. When we reached the rock something fell from it. Pegyal Lingpa put his hand inside the rock, and Khandro as well; both of them were reaching inside a very long tunnel. Pegyal Lingpa extracted something and told me to be ready to take it. He placed something hot into my hand like a white boiled egg – it's very difficult to say what it was made of. It looked like a fruit, but it wasn't a fruit; it looked like a stone but wasn't a stone. It was hemispherical. I held it tightly. Then Rinpoche said, "You must do one circumambulation of Marme Kumbum." So I did one round. Then I told him, "The road is not clear, and if I fall down, we will lose these precious things." So Rinpoche placed his hand on my back to help, and we returned to the site where the rest of the people were preparing tea.

'Inside the white precious object were many auspicious things. There was a yellow scroll, the *chokser*, on which about thirteen texts relating to Vajra Yogini were written; and also some predictions for the future of this world. There was a bell which had belonged to Nub Sangye Yeshe, a previous incarnation of Pegyal Lingpa; a statue of Padmasambhava about nine inches in size, made from a mixture of metals; a Yamantaka statue; Orgyen Dakini's cat made from *zi* stone; and a container for holding seeds. The bell itself is somewhere here, but all the other objects were lost when we were escaping from the Chinese on leaving Pemako. There was also another egg-shaped object made from a mixture of precious stones, like jewels, which was offered to the Karmapa. Out of that the Karmapa took a yellow *chokser* scroll which contained a long life prayer called "Dorje Zandu".'

The treasures that Pegyal Lingpa extracted from Pemako were its spiritual gifts, the essence of what it had to offer. Though he had taken *terma* from Marme Kumbum, the most sacred place of the *dakini*, he could penetrate no further into the hidden land. 'We really wanted to get further,' Lama Setchou told me. 'The local people wanted to give us three years' food and asked to come with us. So we requested a lama, Jamyang Khyentse Chokyi Lodro's nephew, for a sign. He had a dream. In his dream he saw a white rock with a kind of path going up it. On top of the rock he saw a blue woman who said, "No, it's not time to come here yet." That means it hasn't been opened yet. But according to the predictions, which can be found in Taksham Terton's *terma* in Darjeeling, the inner level will be opened soon.'

All the hidden lands have outer and inner levels. Entry to them is not automatically assured for ordinary people, even to the outer level. 'Only fortunate people with a lot of merit,' Thinley Norbu commented, 'are able to go to these places.' Reaching the inner level is even less a matter of will-power than reaching the outer. Acquiring merit means creating the circumstances for the inner level to open. All we can do is prepare.

Since the hidden lands are special places for spiritual development, the inner level corresponds to the inner yogic system and the transformation of the five impure modes of perception (*skandhas*) centred in the chakras, into the five wisdoms. So naturally within the inner level of the hidden lands there are treasures that contain the most potent transformative and regenerative energy: the elixir of life. Accordingly, before the inner hidden land is opened, it lies in a dimension outside time.

Sikkim is a major hidden land where the inner level has been opened. It is where my pilgrimage first began, so when Dodrupchen Rinpoche, himself a great *terton*, placed the precious *terma*, *Guidebook to Sikkim*, in my hands during our first meeting at his monastery in Gangtok, I felt the thrill of auspiciousness, a little taste of the *terton*'s joy when he holds a treasure. It was a sense of fortune, a sense also of the inner and outer levels co-operating to manifest what I needed to know.

The Lhatsun History is a compendium of quintessential instructions of Guru Padmasambhava to enable the *terton* to enter the hidden land of Sikkim through each of the four directional entry points, and to uncover the treasures that he concealed there; instructions at times so arcane that they stir a subconscious level, the place filled by myths and childhood fairy tales. Elements of magic — the invocation of a medium guide, the application of a potion to the feet that can transport one to his destination, a mirror that when polished will reflect all the continents, a demon's hand made of iron that can make one invisible – are mixed with important practical counsel such as a kind and caring father would give his beloved children: be brave, wise, hardworking and co-operative, keep strong commitments within the group, observe religious laws, maintain a high standard of moral conduct, and respect the life of every living being within the hidden land for they are emanations of *dakas* and *dakinis*. In fact, it is essential, he says, when entering the hidden land to practise pure view, seeing oneself as the deity with Padmasambhava at the crown chakra, Vakrasattva at the heart, and *dakinis* as the entire body.

Perhaps the most important instruction, though, is the repeated warning never to attempt entry into the hidden land before it is the right time because it will bring many obstacles. Though Padmasambhava designated Sikkim as a sanctuary for Tibetans during three invasions, it was not until the third invasion of the Chinese in the 1950s that all the signs for entry mentioned in the *Guidebook* manifested. Among other omens, the atheists entered Tibet, the golden spire on top of Samye monastery tilted to the south-west (the direction of Sikkim), black spots appeared mysteriously on Kachenjungna mountain, and a *stupa* was built in front of the Potala.

The opening of Sikkim occurred in stages, each stage naturally bringing appropriate discoveries, until with the opening of the inner level, the essential treasure was revealed. The first stage occurred in the mid-fourteenth century when the *terton* Rigdzin Godemcen recovered the 'Northern Treasure', containing the keys for many sacred places and lands. Later in his life, Godemcen followed the *Guidebook* to Sikkim, also known as *Dremo Shong*, or 'Fruit Container', and entered an abundant valley, a Garden of Eden where flowers, fruits, nuts, crops, sugar cane, mushrooms and medicinal herbs were growing effortlessly. There were precious stones and healing waters. The five peaks of Kachenjungna contained the treasures of salt, of gold and turquoise, of *dharma*, of weapons and of fruit and medicine. Sword-shaped waterfalls cascaded into ponds, sandalwood trees blossomed, and there were more than one hundred lakes with fish jumping into the air. Deer, tigers, bears, leopards and peacocks roamed freely.

There were also strange animals with a mythological aspect which represented the protector-gods of the land: some with two heads, or one head and two bodies; some with a bird's head and four limbs; a monkey with a horn in the middle of its forehead; and animals with twisted horns. These were real animals, and until quite recently there have been people in Sikkim to testify to their existence.

'On seeing this place,' the *Guidebook* says, 'one is suffused with pleasure, and in time it can instil in one a strong faith.' It is described as the equivalent of Bodh Gaya, the enlightenment place of all the buddhas, and Oddiyana, the birthplace of Padmasambhava. It confers such great blessing on practitioners that the benefit of meditating one week here is greater than seven years elsewhere. That is how much easier it is to awaken the inner level in this empowered hidden land.

Three hundred years later in the mid-seventeenth century, the great *terton*, Lhatsun Namkha Jigme, then aged fifty, proceeded on foot from Tibet to Lhari Nyingphuk, one of the five great power places blessed by Padmasambhava in the northern region of Sikkim. There were three important caves there, each with images arising spontaneously from the blessing power of that place. In the southern cave was a buddha surrounded by bodhisattvas; in the middle cave was the form of Amitayus, Buddha of long life; in the northern one was the form of Vajrakilaya. Namkha Jigme opened it as a place of pilgrimage; it was part of the mandala of the inner hidden land.

He also opened the centre of that mandala, considered the innermost level of the hidden land, at a mountain known as Tashiding. It is a wonderful expanse of land, a high-altitude plateau marked in each direction by a sandalwood tree. The central core of Sikkim, its flat summit offers an aerial view of the whole land unfolding from mountain to forest to meadow to river. The inner hidden land is at the very nub of the mandala commanding the supreme position.

The entire hidden land is actually the physical representation of the Tantric mandala of Lama Gonpo Dupa, a central deity with eight deities surrounding it in the four main and intermediate directions. When Padmasambhava came to bless Sikkim, he gave empowerment and instruction on that mandala at Tashiding – the physical representation of the central deity. The inner mandala manifested naturally in its appropriate place, showing the inherent meaning of the outer environment. He also selected a huge boulder that sits on the furthest edge of the summit in the most central position as the concealment place of treasure for the people of the hidden land.

Padmasambhava's bequest in Sikkim was generous and thorough. Like a benevolent father who covers every practical detail of his children's welfare, he buried treasure of every kind, some of it extremely practical and domestic: farming tools, iron pans, earthenware pots and seeds for cultivation. Nine horse-loads of gold and turquoise, twenty suits of armour, thirty swords, and propitiation rituals for the local deities were concealed on the eastern side of a square-shaped turquoise lake. He concealed treasure in many of the nine major and thirteen minor caves of Sikkim.

It was in the major cave of the western direction known as Dechenphuk that Padma placed the most important treasure – a gemstone vase – and issued these quintessential instructions to reveal it: from Tashiding, look west to a mountain shaped like a sleeping pig. Go to the edge of that mountain and look upwards to a very large rock, which is six times the distance an arrow can reach when aimed upwards. In the middle of that rock is a door facing south-west. The interior of this cave is three storeys high and twelve pillars wide. In the middle is a flat stone with the spontaneously arising mandala of Yangdak Heruka on it. On top of this mandala is a wish-fulfilling vase made from gems, surrounded on four sides by four skulls containing nectar and precious pills, together with a *phurba*. 'On reaching this spot,' the Guru promised, 'you will naturally receive the supreme fortune of the great Mahamudra.'

In 1717 the *terton* Ngadak Sempa Chempo revealed the treasure from this cave and brought the precious gemstone vase to Tashiding, to the centre of the mandala. It holds the elixir of life – miraculous water which confers longevity from a special source near Tashiding. Every year a small amount of this water is placed inside the vase and the container sealed. During the year the water increases naturally. On the fifteenth day of the first month of the Tibetan New Year, the vase is removed from it special place, opened, and its water – known as *bumchu* – distributed to all those who gather for a blessing at Tashiding. The people of Sikkim, some of whom live for a very long time, say it is the blessing of the *bumchu*, the regenerative powers of the elixir of life from the inner hidden land.

The unfolding journey into the hidden lands is the process of going more deeply inside ourselves, penetrating the lotus heart of light, until the outer and inner habitats become fused. It starts with a perilous journey to a hidden paradise. Within the hidden land is an inner hidden land – a mountain, cave or lake. Within the inner hidden land is an empowered vessel; and within the vessel is the elixir of life. The journey describes the stages of yogic transformation, the alchemy of transmuting the five poisons of the gross physical body into the five wisdoms through the subtle channels of the body. When this inner hidden land is penetrated, the elixir of life flows naturally, bringing regeneration. Then the hidden valley becomes a pure land, the palace of the Guru, *yidam* and *dakini* – the three roots of blessing and power. The valleys, snow mountains, lakes, caves and trees are actually 'the abodes of celestials, the land of buddhas'. When the inner eye of ultimate reality is opened, we arrive at the Land of Bliss; and therefore, the *Guidebook* says in a final quintessential instruction, 'Very few people can go there.'

Suddenly we are in a non-physical dimension, a field of pure perception. The *Guidebook* tells us that the journey is an essential process, 'purifying the misdeeds of a thousand aeons ... and preventing rebirth in the lower realms.' With the purification stage accomplished and the harmonious balance of the elements in the hidden land, pure perception arises naturally. So all the precious treasure concealed within the inner land is really just to nurture the discovery of our own awakened nature, to help us dissolve the boundaries and reach the limitless lotus heart of light.

Tashiding is like a beacon in the landscape of West Sikkim, an imposing central mountain plateau on which shafts of light seem to focus naturally. It is plainly visible for many miles; yet before it was opened 250 years ago, no one knew it was there. It was physically inaccessible – not because it was buried like an ancient archaeological site, but possibly because it was concealed, like many of the inner hidden lands, in a fourth dimension of space. It was there, but not accessible to ordinary perceptions.

In his extensive research on the Kingdom of Shambhala – a pure land concealed somewhere on this planet – Edwin Bernbaum gives a plausible scientific explanation of how three-dimensional spaces can lie within one another, like paintings stacked against the wall. As long as we focus our perceptions on the top one – on the outer level – we cannot see the others, or even suspect that they exist. 'Just as two-dimensional planes lie parallel to each other in the third dimension, so three-dimensional spaces could lie parallel to each other in the fourth dimension',[3] he concludes. The inner hidden land is always there, but hidden from our ordinary perceptions in an expanded dimension of inner truth.

Perception is always a personal experience. Eleven years ago on my first pilgrimage to Tashiding, the inner level was completely hidden from me. I climbed for an hour up worn stone steps past trees laden with miniature tangerines the size of ping pong balls. Gradually the signs changed. The stone huts became *stupas*; the tangerine balls transformed into huge brilliant letters – *Om Mani Pema Hung* hewn into boulders – and I was standing on a plateau densely populated with *stupas* strewn with prayer flags, looking into the hidden land of Sikkim stretching far below. It was empowering, but strange because I was completely alone.

I had heard vaguely that something precious was there, but I didn't connect with it. And there was no one to ask. The whole mountaintop was empty, as though deserted. I entered a small temple, prostrated to the huge figure of Padmasambhava, made an offering, and walked out into the brilliant sun. It was hot: I had been walking up mountains all morning and I was thirsty. I popped the last tangerine ball into my mouth, and knocked on the door of a simple house nearby. Nothing happened. I began to circumambulate the deserted city of *stupas*, walking slowly in the pure clear heat, letting the cool mountain breeze revive me. I became fascinated by the wondrous variety of *stupas*, each one telling a different story.

Suddenly an old man appeared in front of me. His hair was matted, his clothes were ragged, there were prayer beads around his neck, and he was scowling. Perhaps he was as puzzled to see me as I was surprised to see him. I asked where the precious substance was. He motioned to the small house, and made me understand that it was locked up. He said something about Losar, the Tibetan New Year. Since it was November and the New Year was usually in late February, I thought he was playing with me and dismissed his incoherent babbling with annoyance. It was impossible to get any more information from him. What I understood was clear enough: something was there but I could not see it. I walked away from Tashiding that day, disappointed. The inner hidden land was closed to me; I had failed to connect with it. Perhaps I was not ready to taste its secret essence. It was always in my mind, though, to return.

★   ★   ★

Eleven years later, I do. The setting is the same as before, the same long walk in the melting heat to the *stupas* on the summit. The monastery door is open, and I enter into the midst of a *puja*. I approach the old lama sitting on a low throne with complete confidence, as though we have an appointment to keep and he is waiting for me. It goes like clock-work. '*Bumchu?*' I ask. His attendant returns with a vase covered in a cloth. He fills my tiny container, pouring the longevity water also into my cupped hands. I drink it, cup my hands again, and drink more. Eleven years is a long time and I am thirsty.

His attendant accompanies me out of the door, taking me on a guided tour of Tashiding. He shows me a long rock with the clear head imprint of a serpent where Padmasambhava had subdued a demon that was threatening to destroy humanity. On the furthest edge of the summit, in the centremost position, he points out a huge boulder inscribed with a thick vermilion semi-circle where the door has been sealed. Inside that rock, he says, are treasures for the people of Sikkim, hidden until they are needed. Near the door of the boulder, a fish, a footprint and a dragon have arisen naturally in the stone. Everything manifests in its own time.

Perhaps in those eleven years there has been a process of preparation to allow this day to unfold as it does. My two Sikkimese companions, born and living in the hidden land, have never experienced what we are given today. It is the way everything works, but especially it is the marvellous mechanics of the hidden lands. When it is the right time the door opens, there is food and drink and a guide to show the guest around. Then it is up to him to find the door within and see the inner hidden land.

VIII

O

Dissolving the Boundary

The legend of the inner hidden lands is to be found in every culture. It generally takes the form of a story in which a person wanders away from the established confines of house and home, crossing an invisible boundary into another realm where time has stopped. He enjoys the pleasures of this god-realm, but after what he imagines is a short time, his old attachments arise. He begins to remember the family he left behind and his worldly possessions. He decides to reassure himself by going home briefly, but wishes to be able to re-enter the marvellous realm he is leaving. The immortals who live there warn him he will have to keep a commitment with them, or he will destroy his link with the gods and be locked out of their realm. When he returns to the world he has left behind, he does his best to honour his commitment; but somehow it goes against the flow of human communication. In a moment of unawareness, he breaks it. Instantly, he becomes a stranger in a strange land: the way back to the pure land is blocked. He cannot return and he cannot catch up; for in the human world he has left behind, time has moved startlingly on. Three days have become fifty years, three years, three hundred. He may age in an instant, or become lost and confused.

One example of the legend as told in a different culture is the story of Oisin, the Irish hero who sojourned with the daughter of the King of the Land of Youth.

> Oisin, the son of Finn MacCool, one day was out hunting with his men in the woods of Erin, when he was approached by the daughter of the King of the Land of Youth... The mysterious being appeared to him with the beautiful body of a woman, but the head of a pig. She

declared that the head was due to a Druidic spell, promising it would vanish the very minute he would marry her...

Without delay the pig's head was dispatched and they set out together for ... the Land of Youth. Oisin dwelt there as king for many happy years. But one day he turned and declared to his supernatural bride: 'I wish I could be in Erin today to see my father and his men.'

'If you go,' said his wife, 'and set foot on the land of Erin, you'll never come back here to me, and you'll become a blind old man. How long do you think it is since you came here?'

'About three years,' said Oisin.

'It is three hundred years,' said she, 'since you came to this kingdom with me. If you must go to Erin, I'll give you this white steed to carry you; but if you come down from the steed, or touch the soil of Erin with your foot, the steed will come back that minute, and you'll be where he left you, a poor old man.'

'I'll come back, never fear', said Oisin.

So she prepared the steed and Oisin set off, not stopping till the steed touched the soil of Erin. He soon noticed a broad flat rock, and reached down to turn it over with his hand. Underneath was the *borabu*, the great horn of the Fenians. He asked a herdsman standing nearby if he would bring the horn to him but the herdsman replied he could not lift it. So Oisin reached down to grab it. 'But so eager was he to blow it, that he forgot everything ... one foot touched the earth, and Oisin lay on the ground, a blind old man.[1]

This is the legend of the inner hidden lands, entered in a fateful moment before the time has truly come. 'Never attempt to go there before it is time,' Padmasambhava warned about entry to the hidden lands, 'because it will bring many obstacles. The correct time will be revealed when you learn the quintessential instructions.' Before we are ready to remain in the state of pure being, without attachment, the inner hidden land – actually, the *sambhogakaya* realm – is just a 'trip', a great place to visit but a bittersweet experience.

The hidden valley of Ah Ja Ling lies in the north-eastern region of Bhutan through a twisting precipitous path obstructed by strange trees and unfriendly people. The valley takes its name from a hollow, conical, blue-black rock surrounded by water on which have appeared spontaneously one hundred representations of the primary mystic seed syllable *AH*. This rock represents the essence of the whole place, an archetypal landscape of rocks that all have a hidden meaning. It may be at some point the last place left on earth; so the rocks are impregnated with messages, coded with the meaning of life in an allegorical journey through death and rebirth into wisdom.

It is a valley where great meditators have practised and left signs of their realization embedded into rock: Padmasambhava, Milarepa, Saraha, Shawaripa, Karmapa, the *mahasiddha* Lawapa, the *dakini* Drowa Zangmo, and the crazy wisdom yogi of Bhutan, Drukpa Kunley. Milarepa practised yogic exercises at Ah Ja Ling rock; Padmasambhava transformed his robes into a sheet of stone hanging twenty to thirty feet in the air, as if it had been left on the line to dry. In another rock is a rainbow which marks the place where he had been sitting with Mandarava and Yeshes Tsogyal on either side, his body imprint is on a stone throne. There is the boot of Drukpa Kunley in stone with even the laces hanging down; his bow remains in stone, and the chain with which his dog had been tied is clearly imprinted.

In Ah Ja Ling the mythological element of the hidden lands manifests in an archetypal landscape that is both magical and transfigurative. Suddenly the themes are starkly familiar, as if we had crossed cultures from the Himalayas into Greek mythology. It is the domain of the archetype, beneath culture, beneath conscious mind, embedded in the deepest level where images and themes bear the imprint of primal truth.

The landscape confronts us with regions of the mind, or realms, that we generally do not acknowledge because we suppress them: heaven and hell, the *bardo* of becoming, the fear of death. My guide was Lama Tsering, a Bhutanese lama who had made a pilgrimage to Ah Ja Ling as a young monk eighteen years previously. 'It takes at least five days to make a complete circumambulation of this place and see everything. What you meet on the way are representations of the hells, and also of the pure land,' he said. 'The first things you meet are the cold hells. They are represented by a rock which you have to go inside and down, turning around till you come out the other end. In the hot hells there are three big stones, inside which water foams and bubbles as if it were boiling.' Further away there is another area, a hell realm of sharp weapons, in which everything – wood, stones and even grass – has the form of weapons. 'All the stones here are very sharp and cutting,' he commented.

Amongst the boulder landscape of the hidden valley is a stone shaped like a house with various stages or levels on it. It represents the Copper-Coloured Mountain, the pure land of Padmasambhava – the *sambhogakaya*; a non-physical dimension accessible only to those of pure perceptions. The hidden land is a stage in the journey to it, a place in which to overcome the fear of death and to be reborn.

Within a rock tunnel at Ah Ja Ling there lives a wisdom being, having the power to weigh the virtue and non-virtue of those who enter it. It is a passageway representing the *bardo*, the intermediate state between death and rebirth. It can release or seize and destroy on the spot. It is the moment of truth, and, after arbitration, its judgement is final. 'If you get stuck in the middle of this tunnel,' Lama Tsering explained, 'you have the feeling you are going to die there; you cannot go forward or backward. But if your friends recite mantras or pray for you, and you promise to dedicate yourself to virtue, then the rock will release you. We see the tunnel as a stone,' he explained 'but actually it is a deity. Therefore a fat man without obscurations will never get stuck, whereas a thin man with many obscurations will.'

This is what happend to one sinner on Judgement Day. 'There was a black magician who was harming the *dharma*. He could not pass through this *bardo* tunnel and was dying there. His friends were unable to pull him out, so they left. When they returned the next day, they found his body some distance away, expelled from the rock – dead.' Near the *bardo* tunnel is a stone on which have appeared spontaneously the peaceful and wrathful deities of the *bardo*, images arising naturally from the inherent meaning of that place.

Another stage of the pilgrim's progress in confronting the fear of death is the place where three human bodies have been transformed into stone. The blessing from these stones is so powerful a catalyst in the profound realization of impermanence, that it is said to be equal to carrying a hundred thousand corpses on one's back; and the depth of this realization helps to overcome the fear of death and what lies beyond in the *bardo*.

Lama Tsering told me a story about the remarkable transfigurative energy of this particular hidden land, a story which has a legendary, timeless quality. One day, a cowherd happened upon a lama sitting on a square stone in this valley. He offered him milk, and he drank it and asked the cowherd if he had a wish. The cowherd confessed that he had an overpowering fear of dying, and requested the lama to help him at the moment of his death. The lama gave his promise. When the cowherd died, his body transformed into a rainbow, and all that remained were small, white, shining relics – *ringsel*. He did not know it, but he had had the great fortune to meet Guru Padmasambhava.

So having confronted the dark underworld, and surrendered to the uncontrollable in the *bardo*, there are healing waters that help spiritual regeneration. When Padmasambhava attained realization of the long-life deity Amitayus, a large stone long-life vase materialized. He concealed it to benefit beings in the future. It sits on top of a large rock, water flowing naturally out of both sides, bestowing the blessing of long life on fortunate beings. On certain auspicious days of the month, water also flows naturally out of a stone that represents his horse. In another place is a large rock from which medicinal water and *dutsi*, blessed nectar, flow. The medicinal water is said to heal the hundred different kinds of disease. Nearby are the naturally arising fingerprints of the twenty-one Taras. Elsewhere, a rock with the spontaneously arising mandala of the Medicine Buddha shows that enormous healing energy is manifesting here.

From three stone thrones where the Guru sat with his two consorts, Yeshes Tsogyal and Mandarava, blessed nectar water flows. 'If you pray sincerely here,' Lama Tsering said, 'then close your eyes and put your hand in the water, you may find *ringsel*, a statue of the Buddha, of Amitayus, Chenresig, or Vajrapani.'

From the mouth of a high rock which resembles the primordial Buddha, Kuntuzangpo, water flows into a pond. Behind it is a stone with the bodyprint of Padmasambhava. There is a waterfall here and when the sun shines it forms a magnificent rainbow over the stone imprint. 'If you drink this water, or wash your body in it,' Lama Tsering explained, 'it will help to purify bad karma, to cut off the lower realms, and attain liberation. There is also bamboo grass planted very firmly in the water. You have to have very good karma to pull it out. If you eat the root, it is supposed to cure bodily illness, cut off rebirth in the lower realms and bring liberation. We all ate a little bit of this,' he added.

Inside another stone is the ritual skullcup of the *dakini* Drowa Zangmo. It is placed inside a larger rock and covered top and bottom so that nothing can get inside. 'But there is always *dutsi* coming into the skullcup,' he testified. 'It just naturally produces itself. You can put your hand through a hole and take some. It's not a big container so it continuously refills. Drinking it eliminates obstacles and increases life.'

After journeying through the stages of death and disintegration of the ego, and bathing in the spiritually energizing waters, we then approach the interior of the valley and a different landscape: a grassy plain containing a lake where fabulous treasure has been concealed. 'There are two plains,' Lama Tsering explained. 'One is called the sun plain; the other the plain of the moon. At the edge of the sun plain there is a lake; inside the lake are one hundred golden plates. Within the lake of the moon plain are one hundred plates of silver. These are guarded by a *terdak* [guardian of treasure] which lives inside the lake. It has the body of a *naga* [serpent] and the head of a tiger. You cannot see it, but it is there; nor can you see the plates, but according to the *Guidebook* they are there.'

These treasures are the essence of male and female, sun and moon energies, purified of all dross in to purest gold and silver, then concealed within the subconscious mind – the lake – and protected by the guardian. Only the right person at the right time can claim the treasure. As we step further into the interior of the mind where the treasure is hidden, the landscape becomes archetypal.

'There is another plain,' he continued, approaching the heart of his narrative journey, 'in which there are a lot of rocks – one big one with many small ones around it. It is said that Drukpa Kunley was sitting on this big rock making astrological calculations – his footprints are actually on it. Around him were all the animals [in the zodiac], and they were all transformed into stone. Right now they are in a dream-like state in the form of stones, but at a certain moment in the future, they will become alive and lead a normal life again.'

I was astonished. It was a startling but familiar theme both biblical and mythological. Literal and symbolic truth seemed to melt into one profound meaning in an instant. 'It's some kind of storage,' he explained, in answer to my surprised expression. 'There will come a time when beings are exhausted; there will be no more seeds available for new sentient beings. Stones can never perish, whereas sentient beings can perish in an epidemic or because of some kind of gas which may destroy the whole population. At this point, these beings will automatically become alive. They will not need a seed.

'In another place there are stone people,' he continued to my amazement, 'many people hidden inside stones. They have become *ters*. When they come to life again, there will be 108 lamas, 108 soldiers, and 108 people. Now they are very big stones.'

His words stretched the logical parameters of my mind beyond the boundaries of possibility. 'Can you recognize them as people?' I asked, trying to grasp this phenomenon.

His answer led into the fourth dimension, to the mystery of the inner hidden lands, in a theme that is repeated in stories throughout the Himalayas; repeated in legends, in the mythology of every human culture. 'You cannot see them,' he replied, 'but someone who is staying there for a very long time will sometimes hear the sound of human talk, of people shouting, dogs barking or birds singing, sometimes a horn blowing. This can be heard sometimes.

'Outside the door of this secret land,' he continued, while I listened spellbound, 'there are two stones in the form of lions. These are the guardians of the entrance. There is a rock with the two eyes of Chenresig on it. If you walk underneath it, you come to another rock on the other side, which resembles a door with a key in it. This door is now closed and it is not possible for us to go inside. But this is the door which enters into the inner hidden land.

'The key is in the hands of Padmasambhava, and so far he has not let anyone inside, though the great masters who can perform miracles can go in. The *tertons* have been inside. The human *ters* are in there, people concealed inside stones. Great beings, like Karmapa, can emanate miraculous bodies, so they can go inside and make offerings to these human *ters*, talk to them, hear their voices.

'They are like gods,' he explained. 'It is a divine realm. There is an abundance of everything – beautiful places to stay, food, drink – a god realm. When the time comes, the door will be opened; these beings will come alive, and we'll be allowed inside to greet them.

'According to the prophecy, when the time comes, the people who have a link, a connection with Ah Ja Ling, will come from everywhere. Nobody will have to call them. They will just know the time is ripe and will gather together there – even if they are in America or some other distant place. They will know it is the right time, and will get inside this place without any trouble. Whereas those who have no connection with it, though they may live right next to Ah Ja Ling, will not understand what is happening or find the way in. Even if they see people going inside, they will be closed off with no opportunity to get in.

'When one is able to get inside, however old you may be, there is no more fear of death.' Then my guide to the hidden land told me a story that is as old as the concept of time itself: a story about an inner place where time has stopped, a place with no past and no future, just the timeless present. A 'once upon a time' story about a simple cowherd who, without any preparation, without knowledge of the quintessential instructions, quite simply one day walked into the inner hidden land, and suddenly stepped outside of time.

'This story happened about a hundred years ago,' he related. 'One day a cowherd noticed that his cow was wandering off. It disappeared and returned several times, so he decided to follow it and see where it went. Eventually it led him into this hidden land. He got inside, was offered an abundance of food, and was very happy. He remained there for three days. Then his cow wanted to leave, so he decided to follow it back and to return. The gods who were living there cautioned him not to tell anyone of what he had seen. They said, "You must not tell anyone what you have experienced here, otherwise you will not be able to enter again."

'When he arrived home he noticed that something very strange had happened. Though he had been away for only three days, he could not recognize his children. They had grey hair, like old people, though he was exactly the same as before. He talked to them, saying he was their father, giving his name and calling them by their names. But they did not believe him. They said their father had just walked off with the cows one day and somehow had never returned. "How can you be our father when you are younger than we are?" they asked. Fifty years had passed in the outside world, and he was a stranger in his own place.

'So to prove what he was saying, he started to tell a little bit of his story – that he had walked through a rock and stayed inside it for three days. "When I returned," he explained, "I found that the world has changed so much." By revealing only this much, though, he was harming the blessing he had received from the secret land. When he returned to the rock, it was closed. There was nothing but stones and he could not get in again.'

There were three of us in my room at Sherabling listening intently to every word of Lama Tsering's account. A hush fell as he came to the end of his extraordinary testament. We looked at each other like children sharing the poignant experience of the final moments of a precious bed-time story. There was no more, it was the end. We had to face the dark, go to sleep, dream the dream, become children again. Strange that we had to grow up and travel to the East to become children again and listen with open grown-up hearts to the truths of long-forgotten tales.

Later on, when I was in Manali in the north-west corner of India, I asked Sed Rinpoche to tell me about the hidden lands in the western Himalaya. 'I can't tell you about any particular place,' he replied, 'but I heard stories from my monks who live in Zanskar.

This story happened not more than fifty or sixty years ago, maybe even less than that.

'In Zanskar, near Bardang, there was a shepherd who one day walked away from his flock. He met a woman who invited him to her home for a feast. He went with her and ate some delicious food which he had never tasted before. It never occurred to him that he might be in a hidden land. After the feast he returned, and his friends asked where he'd been for such a long time. He replied that he had been invited by some villagers to a feast. They were sure there was no village in the area he described. He insisted, though, that he had had a feast, and said, "I have brought some for you also." He brought out his cloth, opened it up and looked inside it. To his amazement, there were just stones.

'There are also many stories,' Rinpoche continued, 'of people who go in that region and hear sounds of chattering, or of dogs barking. It probably means that this is a hidden land and that it's not open yet. But somehow, certain people can see it, and some can hear it,' he concluded.

'Does it mean that people are living in the hidden land even before it is opened?'

'Yes,' he replied. 'It is almost like a pure realm.'

Tai Situpa also confirmed this explanation. 'Some hidden lands also have people living there. When they are discovered, you will also discover the people there.'

'Since these stories occur in every culture,' I asked, 'are the hidden lands everywhere?'

'I am sure hidden lands are all over the world,' he agreed, 'but in our texts, which are in our part of the world for our kind of people, it doesn't describe the hidden lands of other parts of the world. But I am sure hidden lands are everywhere.'

Are they all part of the immeasurable activity of the innumerable forms of Padmasambhava, I wonder. Finding clues to them becomes a meditation; something like a state of grace, when just by wishing deeply from the heart and asking, what we need to know is revealed to us. Uncovering within, I discover.

The day before I was due to leave Kathmandu, I had the great fortune to sit at the feet of Thinley Norbu Rinpoche for an hour in his private room, while he revealed the key to the hidden lands, a transmission of their profound meaning. It was late afternoon, a few days after the Tibetan New Year, and many people were waiting downstairs to greet him. But circumstances had ripened and my time had come. He imparted his teaching with heartfelt conviction, with an urgency that made me listen with my whole being.

He answered my unasked question immediately. 'In general, there is nothing in the world that hasn't been blessed by Padmasambhava – not even one horse's footprint. He blessed the whole world with his miraculous wisdom body – it's not like a physical karmic body.

'Many holy places, such as Bodh Gaya, are not hidden, and you can go openly. Anyone can go there, including evil people; anti-Buddhist people can walk there. But Bodh Gaya remains hidden for them because they have no faith. For you and me who have faith in Buddha Sakyamuni, it's not hidden. So for some it is hidden, for some it is not hidden. This is sentient beings' different phenomena and karmic propensities.

'But the places of the Vajrayana masters – the eighty-four *mahasiddhas*, Padmasambhava and Yeshes Tsogyal – those are hidden places even for someone who has faith. Why? Specifically there are twenty-four hidden places and thirty-two precious holy places – the holy places of the eighty-four *mahasiddhas*. Why are they precious? Why hidden? It's because those outer places are connected with inner energy places.

'I need more time to explain how the outward holy places connect with the five *skandhas*, then with your secret wisdom mind. It is the tradition of the inner Tantric teachings, the tradition of the inner yogas to explain how to communicate between the outer hidden holy place and the five *skandhas* and chakras, and then to explain how the five *skandhas* and chakras are related with wisdom mind. Outer, inner, and secret. If you have that kind of information and explanation, then automatically you can believe in the holy places and in your own buddha nature. And you can blossom.

'The main key is that those places are blessed for practitioners. Those holy places are powerful, so by practising there your mind becomes more peaceful, calm and quiet, faith can arise more easily – many positive qualities can arise through those holy places. The benefit is that you will not be disturbed by the negative energy of ordinary beings. Your energy will be balanced. If you stay there and practise, you can increase your wisdom energy and sublime energy. If you have faith and practise seriously, then you can enter into the ultimate state of enlightenment – the *dharmakaya* place, which is inconceivable, with immeasurable *sambhogakaya*'s buddha field. So, ultimately, the benefit is that you can attain enlightenment.

'But you have to connect.' His voice was urgent. He looked at me intently. 'You cannot jump there. It is impossible to go there with the karmic body. You can only go through your faith in this *nirmanakaya* land, through faith and practice with this karmic physical body – using this karmic physical body with faith, devotion and practice, because you need support. Buddha nature blossoms through that connection.

'When your actual wisdom mind blossoms, then your own mind is going to change from an ordinary place to a sublime being's place. But it is not physical, not tangible. It is immeasurable, inconceivable wisdom power. Hidden doesn't mean only hiding something material,' he said with conviction. 'Hidden is actually *inconceivable quality*. So it *is* a secret hidden place.'

'That is the basic idea of holy places, hidden places.' He relaxed suddenly. There had been an intense concentration of energy to communicate something I needed to understand. The inner journey, at a certain stage, had to be supported by the outer journey; otherwise the inner and secret hidden places would remain sealed. It explained the feeling of support I experienced in the East, like being cradled in the embrace of a vast, compassionate mother. The burden of isolated individuality just dropped away and I connected naturally with the mindstream of the buddhas. It was the blessing power of holy places.

He seemed to pick up on my thoughts. 'The energy here is totally different from in the West. Even though Nepal is a very simple country, it is beneficial. Just being in these countries – Tibet, Nepal, India, Bhutan – your mind becomes calm, easy, and somehow more interested in spirituality. In the West, there is a very good life, but it's extremely disturbed. There is no meaning. If you just stay with people and don't practise, pray or cultivate faith, your life goes to ruin.'

I nodded, my heart aching suddenly. His words had touched a tender spot. It was the unresolvable sadness of my life to have a physical body which was comfortable in the West and a mind that could feel supported only in the East. So I had constantly to span cultures and continents to survive. He leaned over, looked directly into my eyes and imparted a last transmission. The outer hidden places are for the inner hidden place. The inner hidden place is for the secret holy place, which means one's own mind. Then if one develops faith and belief in how to communicate with those holy places, then wherever you are, there is the holy place.' He paused a moment. 'Technically,' he added.

'At the moment I can only give you this brief teaching,' he said with great kindness, 'but I'll pray that in the future we may meet and I can give you a more extensive explanation.'

It was enough, and all I needed to know just then. Understanding the connection of the outer, inner and secret levels was the key. The first connection, perhaps the most important one, had been made. Knowledge is like nectar, and I had just had a tiny sip. It expanded my mind, enlarged the vision, allowed a glimpse of the mechanics of enlightenment. It was a magically auspicious journey into the unexplored, inaccessible interior to uncover the unlimited treasure of the mind. The outer journey supports the inner one, because our environment is the container with the same five elements as our bodies. It holds us, conditions us, nurtures us. Supported like this, we can dissolve the boundary between the two and realize our limitless nature.

I returned to Sherabling for a last interview with Tai Situpa. I decided to focus it on the geomancy of power points, the natural aspects of certain places that trigger realization. So I read aloud the quintessential instructions of the *dakinis* to one worthy disciple:

> On one occasion three women approached Zurpoche and made this prophetic declaration. 'In the lower valley of Shang in Yeru ... lies a valley shaped like a half moon. In its uplands there is a rock shaped like a heart. In its lowlands there is a plain which resembles the skin of Matram [Rudra] after he was "liberated". On a mountain shaped like a trunk of an elephant is a rock which resembles the forehead of a lion. Three rivers flow from three mountain springs, symbolizing the three buddha bodies. If you meditate there you will attain buddhahood and serve the world for a long time.[2]

'Do you think that at a certain point everybody will have to go to a particular place to attain realization?' I asked.

'I think so. That's why Buddha attained enlightment. He went to the bodhi tree.'

'So when the time is right for each person, they will go to some *nirmanakaya* hidden place?'

'Well, you can describe anything like that, because everything is *nirmanakaya*.'

'But the hidden lands all have special geomancy, in terms of mountains, caves, rocks, everything.'

'Oh sure, of course, of course.' He looked at me. I waited for him to continue but he was silent. It was my turn again.

'They all had positive geomancy to begin with, and then Padmasambhava also went there and blessed it making it a special place, so do you have to connect with a *nirmanakaya*...?'

'*Right place*,' he interrupted emphatically.

'Right place,' I repeated.

'*Right time.*'

'In order to get *dharmakaya* realization?'

'Yes, of course, of course. The right place can be anywhere. The right place can be the wrongest place for someone else. It can be on a subway, it can be anywhere. It doesn't have to be just an unspoiled tree.'

'It can be anywhere?'

'I think so.'

'Depending on the person, his nature and tendencies?'

'Yes, I think so.'

'So it is a conjunction of all the right elements that somehow comes together?'

'Yes, yes.'

That is the fully expanded view of the buddha mind, the sacred outlook that the hidden lands are everywhere; for when illusory boundaries are dissolved, no place is more sacred than anywhere else. It is a circle and I had just closed the gap to complete it: we go somewhere special to find out there is nowhere to go.

* * *

I need the support of these sacred places. My whole body responds to their vibration, like tuning an instrument to the right key and sounding a pure note. Certain arrangements of boulder, water, trees and mountains have always lured me. For me, certain landscapes are like the interior of a house when the right colours are on the wall and the furniture has been arranged perfectly. When you sit down, you just relax and feel the inner stillness of pure being.

There is now a very small temple on the furthest edge of Khechuperi Lake, but the lake itself and the forest surrounding it have not lost the remoteness of my memory of eleven years ago. I was enchanted then by this place, and so I am now. The primeval forest is still untouched – like the hidden lands of my imagination – with overhanging trees draped with the most elaborate of mossy growths, embroidered with the wildest fungus creations. It shows the natural arrangements of beginningless time; because from beginningless time, no one has ever pruned, hacked, clipped or chopped anything here. The trees are massive with an awesome presence. Magisterial personalities, it would be unthinkable to interfere with them.'

It is twilight when I arrive at this sacred site, the lake blessed by Padmasambhava twelve hundred years ago. There are changes here from twilight into night, and sunrise into day: changes of temperature, moisture, light and colour, with seasons tuned to different shades. But they are cyclical changes, circular movements. There is no progression or regression. Nothing is going anywhere; it just is exactly where it is. Only more so, deeper into itself, its own primordial nature.

I begin to walk, to circumambulate the lake on the barest trace of a muddy cow path, climbing over the roots of trees projecting out of the ground like the cracked knuckles of an ancient crone; catching glimpses of the magic mirror of the lake through lace curtains of moss dripping from overburdened branches; climbing up, and scrambling down in a fruitless attempt to find a clean trail. The path I remember from eleven years before is gone, or else it has become shrouded in gloom. It is nearly night and I realize suddenly that I am lost in the forest, like a child in a fairy tale. I panic and with heart beating wildly, run towards the lake; but as the dark of the forest clears, the boggy ground of the lake begins – a spongey black bog that stretches a hundred yards or more from the forest to the perimeter of the lake.

I am trapped. There is nowhere to go, no path, no way out. I re-enter the dark primordial mansion, find a comfortable hollow in the body of a massive ancient crone, and surrender to the night. I become sensitive to its soft texture, and begin to relax deeply, letting go of tightness. Knots of impeding emotions loosen naturally as I put my old self to rest in the loving blanket of that soft night. So still it is, that when a leaf falls to the ground, it resounds in the forest with a crash.

There is nowhere to go anymore. I sit up and with open eyes stare fearlessly into the face of darkness, till it changes naturally to light.

Notes

CHAPTER 3

1. Dowman, *The Legend of the Great Stupa*, p. 74.
2. Ibid., p. 74.
3. Ibid., p. 74.
4. Evans-Wentz, *The Tibetan Book of the Great Liberation*, p. 109.
5. Ibid., p. 109.
6. Ibid., p. 111.
7. Tai Situpa, *Tilopa*, p. 65.
8. Evans-Wentz, *The Tibetan Book of the Great Liberation*, p. 145.
9. Ibid., p. 146.
10. Ibid., p. 147.
11. Tarthang Tulpu, *Mother of Knowledge*, pp. 30–1.
12. Evans-Wentz, *The Tibetan Book of the Great Liberation*, p. 120.
13. Tarthang Tulpu, *Mother of Knowledge*, p. 7.
14. Ibid., p. 150.
15. Evans-Wentz, *The Tibetan Book of the Great Liberation*, p. 178.
16. Tarthang Tulpu, *Mother of Knowledge*, p. 152.
17. Ibid., p. 121.
18. Ibid., p. 143.
19. Ibid., p. 89.
20. Ibid., p. 89.
21. Sogyal Rinpoche, *Dzogchen and Padmasambhava*, p. 33.
22. Tarthang Tulpu, *Mother of Knowledge*, pp. 148–56.
23. Ibid., p. 127.
24. Ibid., p. 209.
25. Ibid., p. 213.
26. Ibid., p. 151.

CHAPTER 4

1. Tulku Thondup, *Hidden Teachings of Tibet*, p. 135.
2. Evans-Wentz, *The Tibetan Book of the Great Liberation*, p. 178.
3. Ibid., p. 181.
4. Tobgyal, *The Life and Teaching of Chokgyur Lingpa*, p. 50.
5. Nuden Dorje is a previous incarnation of Zilnon Lingpa.
6. Tobgyal, *The Life and Teaching of Chokgyur Lingpa*, p. 21.
7. Tulku Thondup, *Hidden Teachings of Tibet*, plate 6.
8. Ibid., plate 6.
9. Ibid., p. 151.

CHAPTER 5

1. Wilhelm, *I Ching*, p. xxiv.
2. Ibid., p. xxv.
3. Jung, *Synchronicity*, p. 44.
4. Ibid., p. 132.
5. Ibid., p. 29.
6. Ibid., p. 29.
7. Ibid., p. 28.
8. Ibid., p. 142.
9. Dalai Lama, *Freedom in Exile*, p. 55.
10. Ibid., p. 91.
11. Martin, *Bka-gdams Glegs-dam*.
12. Dalai Lama, *Freedom in Exile*, p. 85.

CHAPTER 7

1. Dudjom Rinpoche, *The Nyingma School of Tibetan Buddhism*, Volume 1, p. 816.
2. Ibid., p. 957.
3. Bernbaum, *The Way to Shambhala*, p. 49.

CHAPTER 8

1. Campbell, *The Hero with a Thousand Faces*, pp. 221–2.
2. Dudjom Rinpoche, *The Nyingma School of Tibetan Buddhism*, Volume 1, p. 622.

Glossary

Amitayus: literally the deity of infinite life; the *sambhogakaya* aspect of Amitabha and the spiritual source of Chenresig.
bardo: the state of consciousness between death and rebirth usually described as lasting forty-nine days; can also refer to any gap such as between thoughts etc.
beadie: Indian cigarette made from dark tobacco wrapped in a leaf.
bodhicitta: the thought or aspiration to benefit all beings and set them on the path to liberation. Literally the 'mind of enlightenment', in the Tantric path it refers to the drops (semen) which, channelled upwards, become enlightenment energy.
bodhisattva: literally one with the mind of enlightenment. One on the path to buddhahood is a bodhisattva. In general, a bodhisattva works actively in the world for the benefit of all sentient beings.
buddha: literally 'awakened'. Enlightened one who is a perfected bodhisattva. The Buddha of our era is Sakyamuni who lived in India 2500 years ago. There have been 3 buddhas previous to Sakyamuni; there will be 1000 in this era, which is therefore known as the Fortunate Era.
Chenresig: deity of compassion; the 'patron saint' of Tibet. Sometimes called Avalokiteshvara.
chokser: the yellow scroll on which is written the cipher or very abbreviated key to *terma* teachings which awakens the *terton*'s mind to the complete cycle; usually written in a secret language known as *dakini* script.
chuter: water *ter* or treasure; sacred treasure concealed by Padmasambhava in water to be revealed at a predesignated time in the future.
daka: Male counterpart of *dakini*; Tantric deities who protect and serve the *dharma*.
dakini: female embodiment of a buddha, demonstrating highest wisdom in a female form. There are five different classes of *dakini*, but only the *yeshes khandro*, the wisdom *dakini*, is enlightened.

dharma: phenomenon; also the truth of the Buddha's teachings, the Buddhist path.
dharmakaya: literally sphere or dimension of *dharma* or phenomena; the never-ending, changeless dimension within which everything comes and goes; the essence of everything; referred to as the formless aspect of the Buddha's body.
drigu: curved knife; wrathful ritual object representing the destruction of ego.
dharmapala: *dharma* protector, or wisdom protector of the *dharma*.
dutsi: *dharma* medicine containing relics of enlightened beings, *chokser* or bits of sacred texts ground together with a mixture of herbs. It confers liberation through taste, purifying the subtle channels of the body.
emanation: projection; for example, buddhas can emanate innumerable forms.
gau box: amulet box to contain sacred substances or images. Small ones may be worn around the neck like a locket. Larger ones have a window to show the sacred object inside and are placed on a shrine.
geomancy: literally, making predictions using the earth; the science originating with the Chinese, of siting buildings in beneficial relation to natural surroundings – water, mountains etc – so as to channel natural energies and create harmony.
gongter: mind treasure concealed in the unchanging enlightened sphere of the mind, usually accessed through union practice with a consort.
kalpa: a vast time period or aeon. According to Basham, *The Wonder That Was India*, (pp. 320–1), each aeon or *kalpa* has fourteen *manvantara* each lasting 306,720,000 years with long intervals between them. Each *manvantara* contains seventy-one *mahayuga* (great ages), of which 1000 form the *kalpa*. Each *mahayuga* is subdivided into four ages, the lengths of which are 4800, 3600, 2400 and 1200 Brahma-years of the gods; each of which equals 360 human years. (Referred to in Dudjom Rinpoche, *The Nyingma School of Tibetan Buddhism*, volume 2, p. 98).
Kagyud sect: one of the four major sects of Tibetan Buddhism, itself subdivided into four greater and eight lesser branches.
Karmapa: known as the Black Hat Lama of Tibet and head of the Karma Kamtsang branch of the Karma Kagyud sect of Tibetan Buddhism.
katvanga: ritual trident in general representing the consort, held by Padmasambhava and wrathful deities. On it are impaled three skulls, a vase, a bell, a *damaru* and ribbons flowing in the wind.
Kachenjungna: five-peaked mountain on the border of Sikkim and Darjeeling.
kutshab: an image made by Padmasambhava to represent himself which he empowered by dissolving his body into the image. May be made of clay or bronze. There are five major specific *kutshabs* that he designated as his regents. These five are all made of clay and shaped like teardrops.
ku dung: the deceased body of a realized lama prepared sitting up in the

centre of a mandala for the forty-nine day period of ceremonies marking his passing into enlightenment.

mandala: literally place, or centre and surrounding, of any shape or size. A sacred mandala would be one with a deity at the centre surrounded by a retinue or assembly placed in a significant formation from the centre outwards to the perimeter.

mahasiddha: literally one of great power; refers to an accomplished yogi who can show miraculous powers, who has penetrated the illusion of appearance and can demonstrate its essential emptiness.

mar dung: the deceased body of a realized lama preserved in a large *gau* or reliquary as an object of veneration.

Marpa: the great Tibetan translator (1012–97) who went to India and received Tantric teachings and transmission from the Indian *mahasiddha* Naropa; guru of the great yogi Milarepa.

Milarepa: Tibet's great yogi (1052–1135), disciple of Marpa; spent his life in remote caves and demonstrated miraculous powers.

Mount Meru: the world axis: the mountain at the centre of a world system, ringed by chains of lesser mountains, lakes, continents and oceans. The system described is common to Hindus and Buddhists.

mudra: gestures symbolizing particular spiritual attributes or steps towards perfection.

naga: powerful, long-living beings usually residing in water, often appearing as dragons or serpents; entrusted by the Buddha as guardians of scriptures (the *prajna paramita*) and sacred objects. Their function is often to protect precious *dharma* teachings and objects.

Nagarjuna: the great philosopher-yogi and alchemist from South India (scholars are divided about the period of his life): so-called because he revealed the *prajna paramita* teachings from the Naga Kingdom; founder of the Madhyamika school of Buddhist philosophy.

namchak: literally sky metal, refers to ritual objects – notably *phurba* and *vajra* – made miraculously from meteoric-type substance (before it has fallen as meteors), and concealed as *ter* by Padmasambhava.

Naropa: an Indian *mahasiddha* (1016–1100), the disciple of Tilopa. Renowned for his scholarship, he became Abbot of Nalanda University before meeting Tilopa who put him through twelve hard years of training with twelve tests that resulted finally in his enlightenment.

nirmanakaya: literally emanated sphere or dimension; specifically it refers to the form body of high incarnations who come back to help beings become enlightened, to special sacred images or paintings of buddhas; and to the particular concealed valleys or hidden lands empowered as meditation places.

nirvana: the state of ultimate peace and freedom from suffering of *samsara*.

nimayin: literally not a person, but an emanation who looks or appears like a person.

pandita: a learned teacher or scholar, generally of Indian origin.

prajna paramita: literally 'highest wisdom'. The Buddha delivered a discourse on *prajna paramita* at Vulture's Peak in India, the essence of which is that form is emptiness and emptiness no other than form. These teachings were concealed in the Naga Kingdom and revealed later by Nagarjuna.

phurba: also *kila*; three-sided blade or dagger used ritually to stab and destroy obstacles; associated with the wrathful Tantric deity Vajrakilaya.

raksha: cannibalistic beings inhabiting the Camara subcontinent whom Padmasambhava subdued after leaving Tibet.

realization: refers to all the stages of growth into enlightenment, all the way from the certainty of death to becoming buddha. Ultimate realization is enlightenment. From this point there is nothing further to develop.

ringsel: small round calcid substance that often appears from the cremation ashes of a great master or in other ways from his body while he is alive; it can also appear in sacred places.

saddhu: wandering ascetics of the Hindu esoteric path, usually itinerant in India.

samadhi: the state of meditative or concentrative absorption.

sambhogakaya: literally wealth or quality sphere or dimension: the enjoyment body of the buddhas made of light that appears to bodhisattvas; archetypal spontaneous manifestations of enlightened qualities that appear as the five buddha families.

samsara: the endless cycle of birth, old age, sickness and death based on ignorance, – on the mistaken notion of 'I' and other, and the duality created by ego-clinging.

sater: earth treasure. Sacred treasure concealed in rocks, mountains, images, caves, trees, and in the ground by Padmasambhava to be revealed at a pre-designated time in the future. It refers to any 'substance' treasure: texts of teachings which are revealed through a *chokser* or yellow scroll as opposed to *gongter* which arise in the mind of the *terton* independent of the *chokser*; as well as images and sacred objects.

siddha: one possessing the powers of yoga.

seed syllable: the alphabetical representation of the *yidam*.

Sikkim: one of the major hidden lands of Padmasambhava, bordering Bhutan, India and Nepal. Until the mid-seventies when it was forcibly annexed by India, it was an independent Buddhist kingdom with a lineage of Chogyals or spiritual kings.

Songsten Gampo: the first of three great *dharma* kings of Tibet; he ruled Tibet in the seventh century.

stupa: the Tibetan word *chuten* (*stupa*) means object of offering; contains the relics of the Buddha, so people circumambulate it and make offerings to it. It may be dome-shaped or like a tower with many stages or levels. It represents the body, speech and mind of the Buddha in general; but if divided into three categories, then texts represent speech, images represent body, and the *stupa* represents the mind of the Buddha.

tendrel: literally interdependent connection, which can be auspicious or inauspicious. It can mean action as well as sign. For example, 'Today we are doing *tendrel* for the opening of the temple.'
ter: sacred treasure or texts concealed by Padmasambhava.
terma: sacred treasures or texts concealed by Padmasambhava, which have been revealed.
tertons: incarnations of the special twenty-five disciples of Padmasambhava whose destiny is to reveal particular sacred treasure and texts that were concealed by Padmasambhava to help beings in the future.
Tilopa: Indian *mahasiddha* (988–1069) who received direct transmission of the teachings of Mahamudra from the primordial Buddha Vajradhara.
torma: ritual offering made of clay or flour to represent the deity.
vajra: symbolic ritual object with five or nine points at each end, symbolizing wrathful skilful means for cutting through ego. It also refers to the male part.
Vajrakilaya: wrathful Tantric deity with three heads and a *phurba* as a lower body; invoked by practitioners to destroy obstacles.
Vajrapani: wrathful deity, protector of the Tantric teachings.
Vajrayana: the path or vehicle (*yana*) of the *vajra*, symbolizing indestructibility. Tibetan Buddhism is entirely Vajrayana, which incorporates Hinayana and Mahayana. Sometimes called the diamond vehicle because it can cut through anything, it is the swift and dangerous path of transformation using all the ingredients of the relative world to transform neurosis into wisdom.
yidam: forms of enlightened energy manifesting on the *sambhogakaya* level specifically to guide the practitioner to his essential buddha nature.
Zanskar: a small Buddhist kingdom in the western Himalaya within Ladakh between Manali and Kargil.

Biographies

BERU KHYENTSE RINPOCHE

Beru Khyentse Rinpoche originates from central Tibet. He was recognized by the 16th Gyalwa Karmapa as the emanation of the mind aspect of Jamyang Khyentse Wangpo, the great *terton* who founded the Rime (non-sectarian) movement in the nineteenth century. He is also considered to be an emanation of Manjushri, Bodhisattva of Wisdom; and has incarnated previously as Vimalamitra and Gampopa, disciple of Milarepa and spiritual master of the first Karmapa.

In 1959, at the age of thirteen, Rinpoche left his traditional seat at Nangchen. He has established a community at Mainpat in Madhya Pradesh in India, constructed temples in Menang and Kathmandu and, of special importance, in Bodh Gaya, the enlightenment place of the Buddha.

CHOKYI NYIMA RINPOCHE

Chokyi Nyima Rinpoche was born near Lhasa in central Tibet in 1951. When he was eighteen months old, he was recognized by the 16th Gyalwa Karmapa as the seventh incarnation of the great yogi Gar Drubchen, an emanation of Nagarjuna. He moved to his predecessor's monastery north of Lhasa, leaving Tibet before the 1959 Communist takeover.

Since 1959 he has received personal guidance and transmission from many of the foremost Buddhist teachers of this century, including the Gyalwa Karmapa, HH Dudjom Rinpoche, HH Dilgo Khyentse Rinpoche, Kalu Rinpoche, Thrangu Rinpoche, and his father, Tulku Urgyen Rinpoche.

In 1974 he moved to Baudhanath, near Kathmandu, and helped his father build the Ka-Nying Shedrup Ling Monastery. Later he was made

Abbot by His Holiness Karmapa, taking responsibility for the physical and spiritual welfare of the community of monks. Fulfilling the wish of his teachers, he has in recent years generously given his time and energy to teaching people from all over the world.

DZONSKAR JAMYANG JHYENTSE RINPOCHE

Rinpoche was born in Bhutan in 1960 and recognized as the activity emanation of Jamyang Khyentse Chokyi Lodro, one of the most outstanding Tibetan masters of this century and a leading figure of the Rime (non-sectarian) movement. He completed his training at the Sakya College of Buddhist Philosophy, and has received teachings from some of the most accomplished masters of all four schools of Tibetan Buddhism, including HH the Dalai Lama, HH Sakya Trizin, HH Karmapa, HH Dudjom Rinpoche, and HH Dilgo Khyentse Rinpoche. He is director of the Dzongsar Institute in Bir, India, and teaches widely throughout Australia, South-East Asia, Europe and the United States. He is renowned for his expertise in the various traditions of Buddhist philosophy, and his direct, lively and humourous approach to the teaching of the Buddha.

HIS EMINENCE GYALTSAP RINPOCHE

His Eminence Goshir Gyaltsap Rinpoche was born in 1954 in Tibet and was enthroned at the age of four at Tsurphu Monastery by the 16th Gyalwa Karmapa. He was blessed and crowned with the Red Crown received by the 2nd Gyaltsapa, Tashi Namgyal from the 2nd Karmapa. After leaving Tibet in 1959, he continued his studies at Rumtek Monastery under the guidance of HH Karmapa.

Gyaltsap Rinpoche is the emanation of Vajrapani, compiler of the *tantras*. The first Gyaltsap received the title Goshir – leader of the *dharma* – together with a golden seal from the Chinese emperor, Ta Ming Ching Thung, to signify his kind deeds. The 5th Gyaltsap Rinpoche reconstructed all the Kagyu monasteries and revived the teachings after their destruction by the Mongolians in the mid-seventeenth century. Like the other three eminent heart sons of the 16th Karmapa – the Tai Situpa, Jamgon Kongtrul and Shamarpa – the Gyaltsapas have been the heart disciples and root teachers of the successive incarnations of the Karmapas.

HIS EMINENCE JAMGON KONGTRUL RINPOCHE

Born in central Tibet in 1954, His Eminence Jamgon Kongtrul Rinpoche is the mind incarnation of Lodro Thaye, Jamgon Kongtrul the Great, pioneer of the Rime movement, and compiler of the *Five Great Treasuries*, a precious compendium of the teachings, instructions and practices of all Tibetan Buddhist traditions. He is also the incarnation of Taranatha and Khyungpo Naljor, founders of the Jonanpa and Shangpa lineages. Enthroned by the 16th Karmapa at the age of six, Jamgon Kongtrul lived and studied under the Karmapa's guidance in Rumtek Monastery, Sikkim. During the Karmapa's lifetime he travelled extensively with him and attended him closely. The purity of his devotion to his root teacher has since become a living example in guru devotion and an inspiration to many disciples. He has established retreat centres in Nepal and India.

In his belief that Eastern wisdom and Western knowledge can combine to understand and resolve many contemporary problems, he initiated the Buddhism and Psychotherapy Conference in New York. He also founded the Paramita Charitable Trust and the Rigpe Dorje Foundations in the USA, Canada and Europe to implement projects of educational, medical, social and cultural development, mainly in India. To many who have met him, Jamgon Kongtrul epitomized all that practitioners seek to develop: devotion to the Guru, and wisdom born of loving kindness and compassion.

In April 1992 at the age of thirty-nine, Jamgon Kongtrul Rinpoche passed away suddenly, due to the obstacles for Buddhism, and in particular for the Kagyu tradition.

HIS HOLINESS SAKYA TRIZIN

His Holiness Sakya Trizin is the forty-first head of the Sakyapa Order, one of the four major traditions of Tibetan Buddhism. He was born in Tibet in 1945, and became the head of the Sakyapa Order at the age of seven. From his earliest years, he received an intensive training in the philosophy and the spiritual practices of the Sakyapa tradition. While still a child he successfully completed a seven-month meditation retreat during which he continually invoked the Tantric deity Hevajra. He had seven main gurus, among whom was the renowned Jamyang Khyentse Chokyi Lodro. He has received many teachings from Sakyapa and Nyingmapa lamas, and he is a master of the Dzogchen teaching as well as of the specifically Sakyapa Tantric and philosophical teachings. His Sakyapa followers look upon him as an emanation of Manjushri, the Bodhisattva of Wisdom. His Nyingmapa followers regard him as a manifestation of Padmasambhava.

SEY RINPOCHE

Sey Rinpoche is the son of the meditation master Apo Rinpoche, and the grandson of Tokgen Shakya Shri, one of the greatest yogis of this century.

As the lineage is passed down in the family, Sey Rinpoche is the current lineage holder to the visionary teachings of Shakya Shri. He is also the incarnation of Pema Choegyal, a disciple of Shakya Shri and teacher of many Drukpa Kagyu lamas.

Sey Rinpoche and his yogis in Ladakh, Lahaul, Zangskar and Manali continue the tradition of retreating into the mountains in winter and showing the signs of the 'inner heart' yoga by sleeping outside in the snow and drying wet sheets on their bodies.

Sey Rinpoche was educated by his father and by his uncle, Thuksey Rinpoche, in Darjeeling. From Lama Sonam Zangpo, a close disciple of Shakya Shri, he received the six yogas of Naropa. He studied for four years at the School of Dialectics in Dharmasala. He teaches the students of Apo Rinpoche and Gegen Khyentse in Manali, and is married with two children.

SOGYAL RINPOCHE

Sogyal Rinpoche was born in Tibet and raised as a son by one of the greatest Buddhist masters of this century, Jamyang Khyentse Chokyi Lodro. He was recognized as the incarnation of Terton Sogyal, Lerab Lingpa. After Jamyang Khyentse Rinpoche passed away, he studied with HH Dudjom Rinpoche and HH Dilgo Khyentse Rinpoche. He also studied at Cambridge University and now has over twenty years of experience of living and teaching in the Western world.

He has founded Rigpa Buddhist Meditation Centres in Britain, France, Germany, Ireland, the USA and Australia. He is much sought after as a speaker at international conferences on a wide range of subjects, such as healing, psychology, the environment, peace, the arts and sciences. Widely known for his work in the field of death and care for the dying, Rinpoche has just completed a book on death, *The Tibetan Book of Living and Dying*.

HIS EMINENCE TAI SITU RINPOCHE

Scholar, teacher, poet and artist, His Eminence Tai Situ Rinpoche is respected in both the East and the West as a great exponent of the Buddha's teachings, and for his vision in trying to make compassion and wisdom part of life on earth. He is the incarnation of Bodhisattva Maitreya, and his first Tibetan incarnation, Chokyi Gyaltsen (1377–1448), received the title Tai Situ – Far-Reaching Unshakeable Great Master – from the Chinese Ming emperor Yung Lo. The 5th Tai Situpa was bestowed the Red Vajra Crown by the 9th Karmapa; and the 8th Tai Situ founded Palpung monastery, the main seat of the Tai Situpas.

Born in Derge in 1954, Tai Situ Rinpoche was enthroned in Palpung

Monastery at the age of eighteen months. After leaving Tibet in 1958, he joined the Karmapa and lived and studied in Rumtek Monastery under his guidance until he was twenty-two. He then founded Sherabling Institute in India, where he currently resides, and travelled extensively to teach the *dharma*.

In response to Western interest in spirituality and multi-cultural activities, he founded Maitreya Institute in Hawaii, San Francisco and Paris. He initiated the World Peace Movement for inter-faith and inter-cultural advancement. He is the author of several books. His latest, *Relative World, Ultimate Mind*, has just been published.

TARTHANG TULKU RINPOCHE

Tarthang Tulku Rinpoche is from Tarthang Monastery in eastern Tibet. During his early life in Tibet he received a thorough education in the philosophy and practice of Tibetan Buddhism from some of the greatest spiritual teachers of the East. In 1959 he left Tibet and went to India where he taught at the Sanskrit University in Benares for seven years. It was at that time that he founded Dharmamudranalaya, a press dedicated to the preservation of Tibetan literature.

He went to the USA in 1968 and founded the Tibetan Nyingma Meditation Centre, from which many Nyingma Centres grew. In 1971 he founded Dharma Publishing and Dharma Press, which have published over fifty titles in Buddhist studies. Rinpoche has written several of these works including the renowed *Time, Space and Knowledge* series. In addition, he has edited several volumes, among them the *Crystal Mirror* series, and has supervised the translations of some of the more important Buddhist texts to have been published.

At the Nyingma Institute in Berkeley, established in 1973, Rinpoche has played a vital role in the meeting of East and West. He initiated the Human Development Training Program, a dynamic integration of Eastern approaches to healthful living with the psychology of the West.

In 1975 he began work on Odiyan, the Nyingma country retreat centre in northern California, a centre for the preservation of Tibetan culture and tradition. He has also founded the Tibetan Nyingma Relief Foundation to provide assistance to Tibetan refugees in India, Nepal and Bhutan.

Tarthang Tulku Rinpoche is renowned as a visionary, independent thinker and innovative teacher. His extensive publishing and educational projects have influenced leaders in the fields of philosophy, science, psychology, education and business.

TENGA RINPOCHE

The Venerable Tenga Rinpoche is the third Tenga Tulku, formerly one of the incarnate bodhisattvas of Benchen Monastery in eastern Tibet.

There he received a full education and also completed a three-year meditation retreat. In 1959 he left Tibet, going first to Bhutan and then to Rumtek. During the first part of his stay there, he specialized in the study of the monastic arts – religious music and dance, *torma* and mandala-making. He was then appointed Dorje Lopon (Leader of Vajrayana Ceremonies) of Rumtek, a position he held for nine years until 1976. He has constructed a new monastery at Swyandbud in Nepal, and gives courses at *dharma* centres throughout Europe.

THRANGU RINPOCHE

The 7th Gyalwa Karmapa founded the Thrangu Monastery some 500 years ago and appointed one of his most gifted disciples to be its abbot. This was the first Thrangu Tulku. The present Thrangu Rinpoche, the ninth reincarnation, is the highest of scholars. He was born in Tibet in 1933 and holds the teaching degree of 'Geshe Rabjam', the highest recognized degree among all four sects. He was chosen by the 16th Karmapa to be the personal tutor of his spiritual heirs – the Tai Situpa, Shamarpa, Gyaltsapa and Jamgon Kongtrul Tulkus. He is also supreme Abbot of Rumtek Monastery in Sikkim.

Rinpoche has travelled and taught extensively in the West and is renowned for his ability to simplify and explain the most complex teachings to Western *dharma* students.

TULKU THINLEY NORBU

The Venerable Tulku Thinley Norbu is the eldest son of HH Dudjom Rinpoche, who was the supreme holder of the Nyingma Lineage of Tibetan Buddhism. He is an emanation of Dudjom Lingpa's son, Tulku Drimed Odser, who was an emanation of Kunkhyen Longchen Rabjam and the consort of the precious wisdom yogini Sera Khadro. In his youth Tulku Thinley Norbu studied for nine years at Mindroling monastery and also received teachings and blessings from many saints throughout Tibet. Thinley Norbu Rinpoche is well-known as a writer. His books include *The Small Golden Key*, *Gypsy Gossip*, *Echoes*, and *Magic Dance*.

ZILNON LINGPA (CHIMED RIGDZIN RINPOCHE)

Khordon Terchen Tulku Chimed Rigdzin Rinpoche was born in Tibet in 1922. He was recognized by many high lamas including HH Sakya Trizin, HH Minling Trichen and HH the 13th Dalai Lama. At the age of four he was enthroned at Khordong Monastery as the holder of the lineage of Nuden Dorje Drophang Lingpa. He was also recognized as the mind aspect of Padmasambhava. He studied philosophy, logic, grammar, mandala-making, astrology and the *tantras* under the great masters of his time.

The lineage of Nuden Dorje begins with Shariputra, the foremost disciple of the Buddha, and continues with some notable Tantric adepts: Humkara who received the Dzogchen teachings from Garab Dorje; Khyechung Lotsa, one of the twenty-five special disciples of Padmasambhava; the great *terton* Dudul Dorje and Taksham Nuden Dorje; and in the nineteenth century, Nuden Dorje Drophang Lingpa, who revealed twenty-three volumes of *terma* as well as *dorje* and *phurba*.

Chimed Rigdzin Rinpoche has been professor of Tibetology at the University of Santiniketan in India. On his return to Tibet in 1985 many miracles were witnessed by over 1000 Tibetans and by the Chinese officials there. Throughout his life Chimed Rigdzin Rinpoche has been known for his magical abilities and powers. He is itinerant and teaches in Europe, India and Tibet.

Bibliography

Bernbaum, Edwin, *The Way to Shambhala*, Jeremy P. Tarcher Inc., Los Angeles, 1980.
Campbell, Joseph, *The Hero with a Thousand Faces*, Paladin, London, 1988.
Dalai Lama, Tendzin Gyatso the 14th, *Freedom in Exile*, Sphere Books Ltd, 1991.
Douglas, Nik and White, Meryl, compilers, *Karmapa: The Black Hat Lama of Tibet*, Luzac and Company Ltd, London, 1976.
Dowman, Keith, trans., *The Legend of the Great Stupa: The Life Story of the Lotus-Born Guru*, Dharma Publishing, Berkeley, 1973.
Dudjom Rinpoche, *The Nyingma School of Tibetan Buddhism*, Volumes 1 and 2, trans. Gyurme Dorje, Wisdom Publications, Boston, 1991.
Evans-Wentz, editor, *The Tibetan Book of the Great Liberation*, Oxford University Press, London, 1954.
Jung, C. J., *Synchronicity: An Acausal Connecting Principle*, Ark Paperbacks, London, 1985.
Kloetzli, W. Randolph, *Buddhist Cosmology*, Motilal Banarsidass Pvt. Ltd, Delhi, 1983.
Martin, Dan, trans., *Bka-gdams Glegs-dam*, Indiana University, unpublished.
Sogyal Rinpoche, *Dzogchen and Padmasambhava*, Rigpa Fellowship, Berkeley, 1989.
Tai Situpa, Khentin, the 12th, *Tilopa*, Dzalendara Publishing, Eskdalemuir, Scotland, 1988.
Tarthang Tulku, trans., *Mother of Knowledge: The Enlightenment of Yeshes mTsho-rgyal* by Nam-mkha'i Snying-po, Dharma Publishing, Berkeley, 1983.
Tulku Thondup, *Hidden Teachings of Tibet*, ed. Harold Talbott, Wisdom Publications, London, 1986.
Tobgyal, Orgyen, *The Life of Chokgyur Lingpa*, trans. Tulku Jigmey and

Erik Pema Kunsang, Rangjung Yeshe Publications, Kathmandu, 1982.

Tsogyal, Yeshe, *The Life and Liberation of Padmasambhava*, Dharma Publishing, Berkeley, 1978.

Wilbur, Ken, *No Boundary*, New Science Library, Shambhala, Boston and London, 1985.

Wilhelm, Richard, trans., *I Ching or Book of Changes*, Routledge and Kegan Paul Ltd, London, 1951.

Index

Ah Ja Ling 124–9
Akshobya Buddha 91
Amitabha 91
Amitayus 118, 127
Amogasiddhi 91–2
amrita 22

bardo 5, 84, 89, 125, 126, 127
Beru Khyentse Rinpoche 61, 144
beyul see hidden lands
Bernbaum, Edwin 120
bodhicitta 76, 77, 78
bodhisattvas 30, 31, 89, 95
Bokar Rinpoche 75–7
Buddha, body of 15–17, 20, 22
   five manifestations of 98
   images of 21–3, 24
   wisdom of 93
buddha activity 87, 92, 98–9, 100–101
buddha families 90–2, 94, 98
buddha mind 38, 39, 94, 132–3
buddha nature 1, 9, 12, 88, 90–1, 98, 133
buddhas 13, 30, 31, 83, 85–6

causality 68–9
Chenresig 29, 71, 77, 127, 129
Chinese invasion of Tibet 74–5

Chokgyur Lingpa 56, 57–8, 66, 113
chokser 54, 56, 114–15
Chokyi Nyima Rinpoche 62, 64–5, 144–5
cosmology 15
Crown, Black 29–30, 32, 74

dakas 30, 117
dakinis 30, 31, 32, 38, 56, 94, 110, 117, 120, 134
Dalai Lama 74–5, 79
dematerialization 6, 85–6
dharma 15–16, 26, 39, 41, 43, 45, 46, 87–8, 107
dharmakaya 6, 9, 24, 30, 99, 110, 132, 135
dharma protectors 59–60, 63, 73, 85
Dilgo Khyentse Rinpoche 51–2
Dipankara Buddha 13, 80, 81
Dodrupchen Rinpoche 62, 116
Dorje Legpa 63
Drowa Zangmo 125, 127
Drukpa Kunley 125, 128
dutsi 62, 72, 127
Dzongsar Khyentse Rinpoche 23–4, 71, 88, 98–9

environmental imbalance 108–9

Fortunate Age 13

Golden Age 14
group energy 71
Guidebook to Sikkim 116–18, 120, 128
Guru Rinpoche *see* Padmasambhava
Gyaltsap Rinpoche 72, 93–4, 96, 97, 145
Gyalwa Karmapa 10, 25, 26, 29

hidden lands 106, 111–22, 123–33

Jamgon Kongtrul Rinpoche 28, 29, 76, 82, 88, 93
Jamyang Khyentse Chokyi Rinpoche 23
Jung, C. G. 68–70

Kalu Rinpoche 75–7
Karmapas 26–34, 77
Khandro Tongyal 111, 113

Lhasa Jowo 21–2, 24
Lodro Thaye 80, 81

Mahakala 57, 59
Maitreya Buddha 14
Mandarava 39–41, 49, 66, 125, 127
mendrup 72, 114
mind, nature of 13
Mutig Trichen 17

nagas 22
namchak 63–4
nimayin 64
nirmanakaya 17, 42–3, 78, 110, 133, 134–5
Nuden Dorje 57, 58, 63

Oisin 123–4

Padmasambhava 18, 27, 28, 31, 32, 35–48, 52, 53–4, 55, 56, 58, 61, 62, 63, 64, 66, 70, 72, 95, 97, 105, 106–8, 112, 113, 116–19, 124, 125–9, 131, 132, 135, 136
Pegyal Lingpa 111, 113–15
Pemako 109–16
perfection, thirty-two marks of 15–16
phurbas 61, 62, 63, 64, 88

rangjung 29, 32, 68, 70–5, 77–9, 85, 101
rapne 23
Ratnasambhava 91, 99
realization 134–5
ringsel 48, 78–82, 127
Rumtek 25–8, 72

Sakyamuni Buddha 1, 2, 10, 13, 14, 15, 36, 37, 71, 77, 80, 132
Sakya Trizin 64, 146
samadhi 15
sambhogakaya 89, 98, 110, 124, 132
samsara 12–13, 23, 78–9
Sangye Nyenpa Rinpoche 63–4
Sed Rinpoche 25, 42, 77, 79, 130–31
seed syllables 78–9, 124
Setchou, Lama 111–16
Shantarakshita 43, 44
Sherabling 2, 6, 9, 17–18, 25, 130
siddhi 24, 45
Sikkim, hidden land of 116–21
  King of 26–7
skandhas 132
Sogyal Rinpoche 24, 147
statues, speaking 23, 24, 25, 27
  taking on illnesses 24–5
synchronicity 68–9, 75

Tai Situpa Rinpoche 2–3, 6, 14–15, 18–20, 25, 28, 29, 36, 52–3, 63, 66, 73–4, 78, 79, 80, 87–8, 99–101, 106, 109, 131, 134–5, 147–8

Tantrism 36, 96–7
Tara 23, 24, 32, 70, 73, 77
Tarthang Tulku Rinpoche 84–6, 148
Tashiding 118–22
tendrel 26, 30
Tenga Rinpoche 97, 148–9
terma 28, 35, 43, 45–6, 47, 52–61, 63, 83, 101, 114–16, 129
tertons 28, 52, 54–61, 72, 111, 114, 116, 117, 129
Thinley Norbu Rinpoche 110, 116, 131–4, 149
Thrangu Rinpoche 64, 149
Trisong Detsen 43–5, 66
Tsering, Lama 125–30
Tsangpa Gyare 77
Tsongsten Gampo 21, 31, 33, 73
Tso Pema 48–9

tuk dam 75–6
tulku 30
Tulku Urgyen 13, 80

Vairochana Buddha 15, 90, 94
Vajradhara Buddha 94
Vajrakilaya 64, 92, 118
vajras 61–5, 87, 91, 94–5
Vajrasattva 92
Vajrayana 93–4, 96–8, 99, 132
Vajra Yogini 88, 92, 114, 115

yang 99–101
yeshepa 22–3, 25, 53
Yeshes Tsogyal 31, 43, 45–8, 49, 54, 55, 57, 66, 73, 125, 127, 132
yidams 78, 90, 92–4, 120

Zilnon Lingpa 54–61, 63, 70, 79, 149–50